T0098757

Revolutionize Your Child's *Life*

Life coaching with Peggy Caruso has had a dramatic and very positive impact on my family. Kids today not only face the traditional challenges of growing up, but now have to contend with the omnipresent and powerful influence of technology and constant connection, which ironically seems to isolate them more than ever. Life coaching is helping my children to understand the dangers around them and to develop the skills they will need in their individual, life-long pursuit of happiness. It is a very practical and effective approach. I am very grateful for all of the wonderful changes it has brought into our lives!

—**Margie Guido**

My children and I instantly liked Peggy. She taught my kids valuable life skills for dealing with pressure, self-confidence issues, and the general adolescent problems. She was also a person whom my children trusted enough to seek guidance from on topics they did not want to share with me rather than relying on friends' inexperienced, biased, and unskilled advice. The changes came quickly, and my kids flourished. They have never been so happy. They will continue working with Peggy so that they remain on a progressive, healthy path through life. What a gift she has been to our family!

—**Mary Meredith**

I believe it's never too early to get your kids involved in life coaching. With the few months that I have done life coaching with Peggy she has really turned my life around. She instilled in me direction, confidence, and most important a sense of self-worth. You could attribute a lot of my issues to a few key areas, but if you boil it down into its purest of forms, there are two elements: problems and reacting to those problems. This book aims to recognize and help correct these problems. Peggy has helped revolutionize my life; let her help revolutionize you and your child's life.

—**Adam Wehler**

Peggy's life coaching has turned my daughter's life around. She has taught her how to navigate through obstacles and challenges that have allowed her to become a more confident and stronger person. The positive approach that Peggy used was very effective and has made a few valuable differences in my daughter's life.

—**Judy Parolari**

I have known Peggy for a relatively short time, going on a year now; but it feels like I have known her for a lifetime. We had an instant connection. She is a phenomenal coach and coach instructor. Among her many successes are those she experiences with children. She has a creative way of putting them at ease and building their trust right from the start. In turn, her implementation of tools and processes to help children are almost immediately noticeable. She has an outstanding success rate with not only children but adults as well. Peggy possesses the tools, techniques, focus, wisdom, intent and knowledge to elicit a client's values, goals and beliefs and then is able to create a plan of action and a strategy for success toward a defined outcome or result. I would highly recommend Peggy to anyone as a coach or coach instructor.

—Sharon Engle

Revolutionize Your Child's Life

*A Simple Guide to
the Health, Wealth and
Welfare of Your Child*

PEGGY CARUSO

NEW YORK

Revolutionize Your Child's *Life*
A Simple Guide to the Health, Wealth and Welfare of Your Child

Published in New York, New York, by Morgan James Publishing. Morgan James and The Entrepreneurial Publisher are trademarks of Morgan James, LLC. www.MorganJamesPublishing.com

The Morgan James Speakers Group can bring authors to your live event. For more information or to book an event visit The Morgan James Speakers Group at www.TheMorganJamesSpeakersGroup.com.

A FREE eBook edition is available
with the purchase of this print book

CLEARLY PRINT YOUR NAME IN THE BOX ABOVE

Instructions to claim your free eBook edition:
1. Download the BitLit app for Android or iOS
2. Write your name in UPPER CASE in the box
3. Use the BitLit app to submit a photo
4. Download your eBook to any device

ISBN 978-1-63047-252-8 paperback
ISBN 978-1-63047-253-5 eBook
ISBN 978-1-63047-254-2 hardcover
Library of Congress Control Number:
2014940133

Cover Design by:
Rachel Lopez
www.r2cdesign.com

Interior Design by:
Bonnie Bushman
bonnie@caboodlegraphics.com

In an effort to support local communities, raise awareness and funds, Morgan James Publishing donates a percentage of all book sales for the life of each book to Habitat for Humanity Peninsula and Greater Williamsburg.

Get involved today, visit
www.MorganJamesBuilds.com.

Habitat
for Humanity®
Peninsula and
Greater Williamsburg
Building Partner

Dedication

I dedicate this book to all the children I have coached and for all the children of the world. It is my true desire and passion to assist parents with recognizing obstacles, modifying negative behavioral patterns and protecting their children from harm. It will help them lead a positive, peaceful and successful life.

To all children: I BELIEVE IN YOU!

And to my special grandson, Jordan, I wish you health, peace, happiness and success. I love you… Grammie Girl.

Table of Contents

Foreword

By Bob Proctor, international best-selling
author and star of *The Secret*

It's a real pleasure for me to be working with Peggy Caruso. Peggy has spent years studying human personality—studying why we do what we do and why we don't do many of the things we want to do. We've got deep reservoirs of talent and ability within us.

Revolutionize Your Life *and* Revolutionize Your Child's Life *enable you to set aside some of those things you're just so tired of doing, so tired of putting up with, to let the genius flow to the surface and manifest in results in your life. I want to congratulate you for making a wise decision of getting involved in Peggy's program.*

Revolutionize Your Life *will definitely do exactly what it says. Begin to live as you like by no longer living as you dislike. Peggy is a wise leader. She's a great career and personal development coach, so sit back, relax, and listen very carefully. But understand one thing: Listening to something is one thing; acting on it is another.*

It's through repetition, listening over and over again, that you begin to alter that conditioning that rests deep in the treasury of your subconscious. You'll begin acting on it, and that's when your life will truly be revolutionized. This is Bob Proctor. Now sit back and get involved.

To hear the audio go to:
www.lifecoachingandbeyond.com

Acknowledgments

This book contains not only helpful information to the reader, but my life's passion. Many people have inspired me to pursue my present career and write this book.

My educators: Bob Proctor, international best-selling author, who made me realize where my true passions lie and how to bring it all to the surface with the intent of changing lives. A very special thank-you for writing the foreword, with audio, for my book series, *Revolutionize Your Life*, *Revolutionize Your Child's Life, and Revolutionize Your Corporate Life*. His teachings reinforce my inner strength and provide the faith to persevere. The kindness he extends is a direct reflection of the principles he teaches.

Dr. Steve G. Jones, who provides encouragement to his students to pursue their dreams. He passionately presents the necessary tools to assist you in reaching success.

Dr. Robert Anthony, for educating me about the subconscious mind and for his wonderful program "The Secret of Deliberate Creation." Sharing his teachings of the different periods in a child's life has certainly made a difference.

Apart from the above, in the course of my studies and while writing this book, I have numerous people who have inspired me with their vision and understanding of higher education. Several personal acquaintances have shared their knowledge, guidance and heart with no expectations.

Niccole Lowe who assisted with my web design. I appreciate your guidance and expertise. A special thank you to my social media consultant, Lindsey Hallstrom, who has been instrumental in keeping me focused. Lindsey is very dear to my heart.

I would also like to thank the following for assisting me at every level of my book: Morgan James Publishing Company, who has gone above and beyond with guidance and support. Their team is a valuable asset to the publication of my book. A special thank you to David Hancock, Jim Howard, Margo Toulouse, Bethany Marshall and Angie Kiesling. Also to my PR team at Smith Publicity who assisted me with the launch of my book.

My wonderful mastermind team who have supported me personally and professionally and helped me every step of the way: Mike Mack, Canada; Bob Urichuck, Canada; Sawaan Kapoor, India; Nilesh Rathi, India; and a very special thank you to my team member and friend, Christina Skytt. Christina is very dear to my heart and has shared many failures and successes with me. She is the author of *Power Goals*.

To my students in my Life Coaching Academy class: Judy Parolari, Melissa Mulhollan, Lori Keech, Pixie Edwards, Gina Hine, and Robyn Brubaker, and a special thank-you to Sharon Engle. Sharon is a very dear friend who has played an important role in my life both personally and professionally. We share the same goals, and our lives are mirrored.

A very special thank-you to my mother and best friend, Mary Ellen Bolitiski. She supports and loves me through all of my endeavors. Her love is unconditional, and she has always been a true inspiration in my life.

To my wonderful children, Nicole and Joshua, who have been my rock—always believing in me and providing the strength and perseverance toward success. They helped me realize you are never so near the top as when you hit rock bottom. I love you both, today, tomorrow and always. They are the best children a mother could have.

My very special grandson, Jordan, who continually makes me smile. He is filled with love and laughter and is a direct reflection of the positivity that I teach. His kindness and sincerity have already proven to be a success in his life.

Bob Hallstom, who has been my very best and true friend throughout. He continually supports and believes in me and has been my sounding board and a true inspiration.

To all the children who have come into my life and made such a powerful impact and to each of you who wrote a testimonial for my book. Each of you has been the inspiration for my writings.

To all the wonderful parents who truly care for the well being of their children and for believing in my abilities. Also, for the wonderful, heartfelt testimonials.

I am happy and grateful to all of you. . .God bless each of you!

Introduction

A young teenage boy…he should be able to fight them off, right? But there are just too many. Walking home, they drag him by his hair into a car. Each of them takes turns spitting in his face, punching him in the stomach, and laughing. They drive into the woods, pull him out of the car, and tie his hands behind his back. They make him drink something that tastes awful; he doesn't know what it is. It is so terrible he begins to cry, and they continue to ridicule him. It seems to last forever. They leave him in the woods, and he doesn't know where he is. Eventually he makes his way to a main road, and someone driving by stops and offers him a ride.

The driver helps clean the boy up and offers to take him to a hospital, but he just wants to go home. While they are driving he begins to think about that—home? His home life is just as bad. A father who beats him and a mother who drinks too much—no love from either.

Since neither parent wanted him, eventually the boy ended up in foster care. He had no self-worth, no friends, and was severely bullied in school. Daily he asked himself, "Am I the only one?" The answer is no. Every year in North America alone, one out of every four children get bullied, living lives of quiet shame and misery—and those are just the ones we know about. How many more countless souls face a reality so harsh that sometimes life doesn't seem worth living?

Am I the only one? is a question so familiar with bullying and the emotional impact it leaves. Oddly enough, within the same school district, and almost simultaneously, a sweet little girl the same age was experiencing similar situations.

Two lost children—same age, same school—arrived at a fork in the road. They came from a road of confusion, two lives with little meaning. They had never experienced the power of expression because rejection had left them unable to adapt in a world too big and powerful. They had no emotion, no social skills, and no awareness of how to function in unfamiliar territory. Their stories depict the widespread social issues of abandonment, abuse, and bullying. But how can we function from a heart with no emotion, a lost soul?

In my practice I talk with so many parents who think they know what's going on with their children— that their lives are balanced—but in many cases it's the opposite. Sometimes the parents don't realize their present surroundings are discouraging them as well as their children. Is it sharing custody? Is it your stepchild(ren)? Is it balancing career and family obligations? Is your child being bullied, or maybe your child is the bully? Is your financial situation affecting the well-being of your child? What does your child truly desire, and what talents does he have? Are you helping your child reach her full potential— possibly becoming a "kidpreneur"? How is social media affecting your children, and are they experiencing the dangers of the Internet?

If you can discover what is going on in your life and/or your child's life then you can find a way to correct it. I speak frequently about the factors of success and failure and how to rebuild your empire without seeking permission from others. The same holds true with your family; you can fix it. You can find hope and a solution to your problem(s).

We need to teach our children how to thrive, not just survive. We need to teach them how to break through "the terror barrier"—when you are doing well and then experience doubt and fear. Do you retreat or break through that wall with confidence and faith? It means distinguishing fear from faith. It means the difference between finding life success or barely existing.

The ten chapters in this book will discuss:

Who and what are manipulating your child's mind?

- When we talk about changing your paradigm (a multitude of habits stored in your subconscious mind), as adults we realize the complexity of changing habits that have been impressed upon our subconscious minds for years. Therefore, we must realize it is much easier to change a child's way of thinking because of the timeline. Identifying where the negative displacements come from allow us to make positive changes in thinking and behavior.

- Comprehension of the different periods throughout a child's life will assist you in knowing where they focus things in their mind. You as a parent can prevent many negative situations just as you can use many positive situations to build upon and strengthen areas of the mind; this will prevent negative outcomes.

How to teach your child the importance of visualization.

- We were taught as children not to dream; but it is much easier for children to daydream than for adults. It can be beneficial. Working with them on the visioneering process is easier than with adults because children are young and impressionable and it can be fun. A creative imagination can make positive changes within your child and assist in setting and reaching goals.
- You will learn the importance of a vision board and how it can accelerate the process of setting and reaching goals. Once imprinted on the screen of the mind it is easier for it to become a reality. In the visualization process one needs to have

his mind calm and clear. Teaching your children techniques that will calm their minds will also prove to be a health benefit.

What do your children desire, and how can you help them get there?

- Once you work with your children to figure out their "burning desire" you can begin the mapping process. We are all conditioned to believe that children can't know what they want, but the importance lies with knowing the desire doesn't have to be life-long. It means creating a way to teach them about desire and allows a temporary solution for keeping them occupied in a positive manner.

- Desire will assist them with commitment, focus and organization. It will also help them reveal what lies deep within them relative to passions, talents and abilities.

What happens to your child when intuition and faith are applied?

- If you believe in a higher power it serves as a power for good. Children, like adults, can learn to develop their own intuition and use it for the rest of their lives.

- You will learn what the impact of faith, or the lack of, will do for your children. Once they comprehend there is a higher power it changes their behavior. They then realize they have to answer to someone or something else. If they believe nothing is higher than the parent then nothing else will hold them accountable for their actions.

Divorce, separation, stepchildren, bullying...HELP!

- Divorce plays a vital role in the daily complications of parenting. When multiple step-situations occur a lot of emotion, negative and positive, results. But once we identify the problematic source we can begin to improve the circumstance.

- Bullying takes place at many levels. Educating ourselves on the signs and symptoms can aid in prevention. You will know what to look for and correspond it to what period your child is in. You will become educated on tools and techniques, relative to technology, that will allow you to safeguard your child from dangers on the Internet and with social media.

Show your child how to persist.

- In this day and age it is easy for us to fall under the spell of procrastination so that the inevitable happens. Children pick up habits from those around them. The power of countering procrastination with persistence teaches children at an early age that they will prevail if they push forward.

- You will be educated on the steps that will lead you and your child to form the habit of persistence and which ones to avoid that cause the lack of persistence.

The powerful outcome of gratitude.

- When I teach children to focus each day on gratitude, they are better able to overcome negative thoughts and are happier in every-day life.
- Being grateful helps them reach deep into their hearts. It will have a profound effect on their future. I give many suggestions to help them be creative with gratitude. It will teach them the power of giving.

What is the real potential of your child?

- Do you really know what talents and abilities lie deep within your child? I thought I knew what my coaching student's abilities were until I performed a discover-your-skill-set exercise and was astonished at the outcome. This is the road to develop entrepreneurial skills within your child.
- It will assist them with the goal-setting process and teach the importance of skills versus passions. I will educate them and the parent on the 4 Cs— skills that are needed for success in education, career and life.

How to turn your children into "kidpreneurs" and teach them the power of masterminding.

- Once you know your children's abilities you discover the direction in which they need to go to place them in the business mindset. It keeps them focused and allows them to experience the wonders of being successful.

- They will learn financial matters they can use from the teenage years into adulthood. They will incorporate the value of working with like-minded individuals into business as an adult. Assisting them with choosing their own mastermind team will enhance social skills. It can provide successful results in their personal lives and with business.

Working together to create successful results.

- You will be able to comprehend the emotions of your children, discover the ways they sabotage themselves then begin making positive changes.

- They will be able to visualize their goals, discover their hidden talents and abilities, learn how to reveal their burning desire, then back it with faith and gratitude. They will learn the importance of finance and masterminding with like-minded individuals. This structured plan will assist them in reaching their desired outcome of success and happiness.

How did the principles contained within this book help the two children I mentioned in the beginning of the introduction? The first child was bullied to the extent of injury and came from an abusive home with no love from either parent—ultimately they discarded him. The second child was bullied by groups of children who inflicted bodily harm and death threats.

Both children had to be homeschooled for the remainder of the year, and once they were ready to go back into the school system arrangements had to be made for an alternate school. They are withdrawn and socially quiet—a byproduct of the negatives they endured—but both children have outstanding qualities, such as good values and a high intellectual level, and both are well behaved.

What is the emotional damage incurred from such abuse? Loss of self-esteem, no empathy toward people or animals, anger, hatred, fear, worry, doubt—all negative tendencies. Sometimes children internalize their negative emotions, which can lead to cutting and hurting other people or animals—and even criminality.

One of the children went to a foster care family, and the other remained with their parent. Later I worked with each child and tried repeatedly to change the way they were programmed. I utilized neurolinguistics programming (NLP), hypnosis, life coaching tools and techniques, and then incorporated entrepreneurial skills. The application of the information in each chapter assisted with positive changes and preventative measures. I strive to reprogram their subconscious minds, and even though it is challenging we are making progress. But the question remains: How do we teach love, hope, and emotions after many years of negative treatment? Whether we are an adult or a child, we all need to light the fire in our hearts.

When the children first came to me for help there was no hugging, no kissing, and, sadly enough, no laughter. After one year of teaching the power of the subconscious mind, dreaming/visioneering, goal setting, and discovering skill sets, we are on the road to recovery. One child is developing entrepreneurial skills and building a business. I discovered *many* talents within each of them and was able to provide awareness of their potential. I am continually implementing techniques to teach the power of emotion that was missed as a small child.

After many long months of coaching, one of the parents shared a story. He had to go on a business trip, and when leaving he gave his child a hug and kiss as always, with the anticipated simulation of withdrawal. No return of affection. Then all of a sudden it was there—an embrace of the heart, a kiss with meaning, and a genuine I'll-miss-you look.

Whether it's an adult or a child, never give up hope on reconditioning beliefs, creating emotion, and establishing a life with new meaning, new beginnings. It's never too late if you care. When you give without expecting something in return, the rewards are beyond your imagination. The look in someone's eyes and the warmth of their heart when you've made a difference in their life will change yours.

Open up your mind and get excited!
It's time to. . .
REVOLUTIONIZE YOUR CHILD'S LIFE!

Chapter 1

Who And What
Are Manipulating
Your Child's Mind?

Children are great imitators. So give them something great to imitate.
           —**Anonymous**—

Booed from the podium when he first released his ideas and was considered an outcast by his peers and the scientific community.
           —**Sigmund Freud**—

He didn't speak until he was four years old and couldn't read till he was seven. His parents thought he was sub-normal. He was expelled from school, and his teachers described him as mentally slow, unsociable and adrift forever in foolish dreams.

—**Albert Einstein**—

Chasing her down the road, the two boys are running very fast, faster than she can run. Her heart is pounding rapidly, and fear overcomes her. She falls to the ground. They pick her up, hold her tightly and force her to drink some liquid mixture. She swallows a big drink and immediately vomits. What was it? It was a combination of urine, oil and gas. They then throw the mixture all over her body. They push her to the ground and walk away, laughing and calling her names. Who would do such a thing, and what impact would that have on the child?

This story is just a brief synopsis of a horrible but true reality. Is it a case of bullying, or is it far more severe? What is embedded deep within the subconscious mind that would allow someone to perform an act that would have a severe impact on the mental and physical well being of a child?

As noted in the introduction, all parents should ask themselves: Is your child bullied, or is your child the bully? Do you know? Scenarios such as the one above leave an imprint on a child's mind and heart. They cause fear, doubt and worry and leave internal scarring. How do we ever eliminate such behavior? Well, first, we must understand the mind and how it works. We must also know how to modify behavioral patterns and be aware of what is really going on with our children.

The event reported above makes us look deep within the minds of the children who inflicted such harm. It is evident they have no empathy toward others. They lack compassion; what has been planted in their subconscious minds will pave the way for their futures. Even though they carried out a harmful act the beliefs in their minds can be changed.

The two boys grew up to be good, compassionate people, and later the little girl, also grown up, asked them if they felt remorse for their actions. Their response indicated that at the time it was a horrible act of bullying; they admitted they had reflected on it through the years. What would make them do it at the time? It depended on the period of their lives, what was planted up to that point and what possessed them to make changes within.

In many instances bullies grow up with their own mental torment. In some instances, however, the bully grew to be worse.

What are some of the things that affect a child's way of thinking?

As we will discuss in the following chapters multiple occurrences manipulate a child's mind. To better determine what factors play a key role you must be able to identify the saboteurs and then be able to fully comprehend how the subconscious mind works.

- Divorce/separation
- Living with step-parents/brothers/sisters
- Bullying
- Social media
- Family/friends
- Technology
- TV
- Video games and the like

For you to understand manipulation in your child's mind you must first understand the complexities of the subconscious mind. Failure to do so can produce negative results, whether it is conditioning or behavioral.

I have read scientific articles that tell us we use only use ten percent of our brain on a conscious level. We use the other ninety percent at the subconscious level. Those who study neuroscience tell us left- and right-brain functions are present throughout our brain. Other experts argue the two have definite distinguishable characteristics.

Your conscious mind is the one that makes choices, or the reasoning mind. It can only be concerned with or hold one single thought at a time. The conscious brain, also known as the left brain, is logical, thinking, analytical and deliberate. It is our waking brain. It is the one that says, "Don't touch the stove! You'll get burned." The left-brain functions help us deal with the daily stresses of life.

When you desire a conscious change in your life your conscious mind exerts a lot of energy in trying to make that change; however, the subconscious mind is the one that has been programmed. Our subconscious mind, also known as the right brain, automatically regulates aspects of us like breathing, sleeping and dreaming. It is our sense of inner knowing—our experiential selves. Your subconscious accepts what is impressed upon it or what you consciously believe. It does not reason like the conscious mind, and it makes up the majority of the total mind's capacity. It absorbs every single detail, and this is why children imitate behavioral patterns of family and close friends.

It is believed that the subconscious mind is shaped between the ages from birth to six. All information acquired between those ages is automatically accepted to be true. The information is then evolved into beliefs, habits or mindsets. This is your paradigm.

How does it all begin?

I've learned about the different levels in a child's life from a combination of my own research and Dr. Robert Anthony, *"The Secret of Deliberate Creation."* From the time a child is born until the age of six he or she is in a stage called the **IMPRINT LEVEL**. This is the level in which sensory information is constantly being imprinted onto the subconscious mind—in other words, information that is being absorbed from the environment.

Remember: Ideas and habits are established from the parents, family, and the like, so no ideas are in the beginning of a child's mind. Therefore, there is no critical factor in children. If you tell them the sky is purple they would have no reason to doubt you because that idea has not been formed in their subconscious mind.

So what does that mean?

What is the **CRITICAL FACTOR?**

Let's discuss this in greater detail. I've studied this important mechanism in our minds called the critical factor, which protects ideas in the subconscious mind. The critical factor compares information you had stored in the subconscious mind. For example: if someone tells you the ocean's water is red and snow is black, there is a resistance that internally says, "No, it is not." When the subconscious mind found this information to be different from what was previously there it rejected the new information. The information does not have to be true or false; it just has to be different from what you already know in order for there to be a rejection. Therefore, if a person decides to make a change, he does his best to make those changes consciously; but the critical factor blocks many of those suggestions for change because it doesn't presently exist in the subconscious mind. You must access the subconscious mind. It doesn't mean change won't occur; it simply means it is a difficult process.

Since the imprint level is so important because there is no critical factor, then what happens if you tell children they are stupid, ugly, fat, and so on? That will be their outlook on themselves. It is negative programming and will determine the outcome of their core being. Can you imagine if you continually plant positive images, such as being smart, pretty, and healthy? I always discuss with parents the importance of autosuggestion.

One way to plant positive messages is to whisper in their ear while they are sleeping. Telling them they are smart, pretty, healthy every chance you get will have a positive impact on their self-image. The subconscious mind never sleeps so even though your child is asleep the subconscious mind is retaining the information.

The child will grow to have good self-esteem. He/she has no choice but to believe you so there is nothing to block suggestions. Therefore, you can program children at a very early age. YOU can affect their future.

What is the next stage?

From ages seven to fourteen a child is in the next level, the **MODELING PERIOD.** This is when children model and imitate behavior from parents, family, friends, celebrities, movies and videos.

You see, we were at times left with confusion, requiring us to figure out why we do certain things or think a particular way. As children, we observed our peers (that is, family, teachers, parents, and the like), and this is how our way of thinking was formed. We even drew on the negative outlooks in life if they were our parents' point of view.

In my coaching business I find that this period is where the problems begin to occur. Other classmates and friends influence children as well, and this is where their self-esteem is affected most. When parents bring their children in for coaching during this period, I find it easier to help them deal with the negative influences (that is, bullying, puberty, and so on). I've seen comments on such topics as acne, weight, and monetary items have a significant negative influence.

I also coach individuals who come to me in their early twenties. The issues I see stem from the negative occurrences that happened while they were in the modeling period. All the stages of life are important, but pay special attention to behavioral changes during this period. It will indicate what they are experiencing and pave the way for the outcome into the next period.

Look for changes, such as how much time they spend alone or in their room, who their friends are, what their interests are, what kind of verbiage they use, and how they interact within the family. It is difficult for parents to comprehend if there are changes in their children due to their own life stressors of business and time management. When children have good grades and seem well behaved parents assume they are doing well.

Changes can stem from a loss of communication, prevalent in today's society. Communication has diminished because of social media and technological advances. This can leave the child more advanced technologically than the parents, which creates the unknown.

What are some suggestions?

Subconscious learning allows youngsters to use information efficiently. One good method to encourage subconscious learning at a very young age is through the use of play, which should be implemented in the modeling period. Most play requires the use of multiple senses, which will trigger the right-brain functions and subconscious learning.

How do we reach our children's subconscious minds during this period? Unlike our conscious minds, which regulate linear thinking, such as teaching our children lessons ("Don't touch the electrical outlet!" or "HOT— don't touch!"), our subconscious minds respond best to creative play. We can access our children's subconscious minds through things like:

- Storytelling: ones that demonstrate good values.
- Songs and music: ones that have good lyrics. This is very important because autosuggestions placed into the subconscious mind have a big influence. Bad or negative words will cause complications. This is difficult for parents to control because of technology; so I encourage you to educate yourself on any devices you purchase for your child.
- Metaphors: this is where you could learn and implement NLP (neurolinguistics programming) techniques, which deal with behavioral modification. You would need to discuss this in greater detail with someone who is educated in the process. This is very successful, especially with children, because many tools and techniques can be applied. It is effective and easily taught to parents so they can assist in the application of the process.
- Rhyming: be expressive.

- Repetitiveness: this is key toward autosuggestion and will implant positive affirmations on a continual basis.

- Hypnotherapy: this is an effective tool with children. It assists with ADD/ADHD, anxiety, weight loss, and so on. As with NLP, hypnosis needs to be discussed with a professional. It may be misunderstood. The therapeutic value can be life altering and accelerate behavioral changes. It can plant positive messages into the subconscious mind every day for a minimum of thirty days. It is intended to relax one's body and mind. It can be effective and utilized by everyone. It is safe and you are always in control during a hypnotherapy session. Hypnosis is proven to be more effective and works more quickly than traditional talk-therapy or psychoanalysis. In a hypnotic state, you are more receptive to new ideas and you can more effectively process the emotions linked to the experiences. It is a special form of communication to the subconscious mind. I use it with children, teens and adults. Many business clients use it as a tool to aid in learning calmness of mind.

The child then moves into the next level.

From ages fourteen to twenty-one the child moves into what is known as the **SOCIALIZATION PERIOD**. This is when he determines unconsciously what is important to him. He breaks away from the modeling period and becomes INDIVIDUALIZED by beginning to form his own identity. Most children in this period still follow the crowd because they want to fit in. They are unaware that they are creating their own reality and habits in the subconscious mind, and this can be dangerous. That is why we are still living out our paradigm—our many behavior patterns that result in habits stored in our subconscious minds since childhood. The habits follow us into adulthood. We choose to follow that behavior because it is our reality and believe it to be true. It is familiarity.

Children who possess strong positive beliefs create a wonderful life and contribute positively to others. This inner belief builds strong self-esteem, which will allow them to navigate through their teenage years with positivity. When children become teenagers they tend to break away from their parents and test the waters. This is part of the socialization period. If they have a strong inner sense they will make positive choices. This will help them avoid the problems of peer pressure, drugs, bullying and other destructive behaviors.

On reaching adulthood we sometimes need to change our paradigm if we are not receiving what we want in life. We all have limiting beliefs from our pasts. Become aware of what yours are and change the ones that no longer serve you. Ask yourself if your belief is moving you toward your goal or away from it.

Your subconscious mind cannot differentiate positive from negative, good from bad. Therefore, it will accept your suggestions without controversy. It is subjective. It is the soil in which you plant the seed. Just as your conscious mind can be thought of as the gardener, planting seeds, your subconscious mind can be thought of as the garden or fertile soil in which the seeds germinate and grow. If a farmer plants poison on one side and good seeds on the other, cultivating the land in the same manner, then watering and caring for them the same, what will be returned? Yes, that's right: poison on one side and good on the other. Well, your mind is the same. What you plant will be returned; therefore, be careful what you think about. If you want flowers and you manifest rocks, you are planting the wrong seeds.

Your mind is conditioned; so when you attempt change you will get resistance. Your subconscious mind is your protector, fight or flight, and guards what has been planted. Change is scary and unfamiliar and difficult. It can cause stress, worry, fear, discomfort, doubt, anger or anxiety.

How does it all really work?

Your brain receives every thought you have. It's subject to filtering, reasoning and logic based on your programming. Once the conscious mind has decided if the thought is true, it reaches the subconscious mind and then is delivered to your life. It's no longer subject to argument. It can only agree with what it knows to be true.

Whatever we plant in our subconscious mind and nourish with repetition and emotion will one day become a reality.

—**Earl Nightingale**—

Whatever was planted in your subconscious mind in your childhood is known to each of you and passes along to your children. How many of you experienced negative phrases such as:

- "You can't…."
- "You'll never amount to anything…."
- "You're going to be bankrupt…."
- "You're going to get sick…."
- "Money doesn't grow on trees…."
- "Money is the root of all evil…."

Those are all negative impressions planted in your mind in the past. They can cause behavior patterns that lead to failure in your personal and professional life. Replace them with positive phrases such as:

- "I can…."
- "I will…."
- "I am successful…."
- "I am wealthy…."
- "I am healthy…."
- "There is enough money…."
- "Money is good…."
- "I love myself…."

You see, you sabotage yourself with statements. Let me give you a few examples of a sabotage statement:

- "I want to lose weight, but I can't stop eating and I hate exercising."
- "I want to get good grades, but I can't get myself to study."
- "I want to exercise, but I just can't get started."
- "I want more money, but I can't find a job."

Notice what's common about all these self-sabotage statements? They all have the word "but" after we state what we want. When you put a "but" after any statement it negates what you said before it. What you say after the word "but" is what you really believe on a subconscious level. We need to examine our beliefs to see if they serve us or harm us. The key is to identify our self-talk so we can work on changing it. In self-talk it is beneficial to keep making positive affirmations.

Do affirmations really work?

Absolutely. Our self-talk contains constant affirmations or statements reflecting our beliefs and attitudes. Constant affirmations become imprinted on our subconscious mind. Our constant thoughts either create what we desire or prevent us from having what we desire. When affirmations are repeated with emotion they begin to overlay what was there before.

I needed to accelerate change in one of my coaching clients who is ten years old so I made her a hypnotherapy tape. I also incorporated positive affirmations in the script. Below is her testimonial for me about a tape I made.

Peggy is amazing! She has helped me in many ways. She has taught me how strong my subconscious mind can be. She recorded a tape for me and loaded it onto my iPad. I listen to it every night. She said, "The tape relaxes you, so it's okay to sleep while it is playing; your subconscious mind still hears the message and records it!" It is so cool! So the next day I am very happy because of the positive messages.
—**Michaela**, ten years old—

I always teach my clients to back their desire with emotion, and that's what I did with her. Almost all self-help books teach you to back your desire with faith; but, sadly enough, there are those who have no faith. Backing it with emotion can create faith. You need to get internally excited about your desire and believe it will happen. I also teach them to utilize their senses and incorporate them into their desire.

As we grow older, our minds establish our identity and way of thinking based on what we have heard and seen from others. Thus, in reality you are the sum total of all the thinking of your past, and you formed your own ideas of success and how life should be based on previous experiences. Just a quick example: I'm sure it's been planted in your mind that you must work hard to make money. This causes a lot of stress for people in their present positions; if they're not working hard enough they feel that they are not doing a good job. On the contrary, many people make a substantial amount of money doing very little. It means you don't have to kill yourself to be wealthy or successful. You don't have to work harder; you need to work smarter.

As parents, if we give our children good beliefs that empower them, then these subconscious beliefs are likely to help our children throughout their lives. As a result, the chances of the children being successful, happy and confident will be high. It is an interesting power to embrace and understand as we help our children establish happy lives.

> *Children need the freedom and time to play. Play is not a luxury. Play is a necessity.*
> **—Kay Redfield Jamison—**

If you read this book in its entirety you will also be able to bring about positive changes in your own child.

Now you understand the complexities of the subconscious mind and can determine who and what are manipulating your child's mind. What's next? You need to see it to make it a reality.

Chapter 2

How To Teach
Your Child The
Importance
Of Visualization

Believe as a child believes, and the magic will find you.
—Teresa Langdon—

He was fired by the Kansas City Star newspaper for lack of imagination and creativity.
—Walt Disney—

A professor suggested he drop out of the English department at college all together. At his first job he was paid in cases of shaving cream, soda and nail clippers. His first book was rejected by twenty-seven publishers before a friend of his accepted it.

—**Dr. Seuss**—

A story of two sisters, Dominique, twelve, and Brittany, nine, who created a vision board aired on an Oprah Winfrey show.

"The law of attraction is a way of life. The way you think. The way you react to situations," Dominique says. "If you're a positive person, you get positive results. If you're a negative person, you get negative results."

"On my vision board are some of my long-term goals," Brittany says. She's included things like becoming a fashion designer, visiting the Great Wall of China and meeting Johnny Depp.

Dominique says the law of attraction is good for more than just long-term goals. "During school I try to keep a positive attitude with my friends," she says. "I notice that if I'm negative, then I'll attract negative things and negative people during the day. So I try to keep a positive attitude." Her vision board includes places she would like to go in her life, like Rome and England, and people she wants to meet, like the Dalai Lama. One of her vision board goals just came true. She wanted to be on *The Oprah Winfrey*

Show. Isn't that amazing? She had the Oprah sign (O) on her board.

Based on that particular story, I am sure you are asking two questions.

What is the law of attraction?

Everyone's perception of the law of attraction varies. In summary what you put out there is what will come back to you, positive or negative. It is a metaphysical new thought or belief that like attracts like. It is visualization, spirituality, quantum physics and energy flow.

Scientifically it would be conceived in the areas of energy and quantum physics. Quantum physics is a branch of science that deals with discrete, indivisible units of energy called quanta as described by the quantum theory. It shows us how we are part of one continuous energy field that we affect with our thoughts, literally creating matter out of light energy.

Albert Einstein was a theoretical physicist who developed the theory of relativity and mass energy equivalence. His most famous equation is E=mc2. That equation, written in that form, immediately suggests the possibility of converting small quantities of mass into large quantities of energy.

He wanted to explain the existence of mass, of matter— simply put, our entire existence. Different forces govern our universe scientifically. Examples of two of these are gravity, which holds planets together, and electromagnetic force, which holds tiny particles like atoms together. The development of his theory of relativity is one of the most groundbreaking scientific breakthroughs of all time.

In chapter 4 I discuss the law of vibration, which is the law of attraction. Your thought controls the vibration your physical body is in. The law of attraction will deliver what you are thinking about.

The second question is: What is a vision board?

Visualization And Vision Boards

Visualization is also known as visual guided imagery. This technique uses the imagination to slow down chatter of the mind and reduce negative thoughts and worries. Vision boards are fun at any age, and it can be beneficial to do them together. The first step is to dream and clearly define your goal in your mind. Make it real by utilizing your senses. Write it down and stay focused; then work on creating your vision board. When you do this with your child/teenager try to be creative.

A vision board is your board of dreams that plants the image in your mind. You find pictures of what it is you truly desire, and then you cut them out and place them on a board. You continually look at this board, and it helps accelerate your desire.

You can use poster, cork, or any type of board in which you can glue, tape or pin your pictures on. Jack Canfield, author of *Chicken Soup for the Soul*, has created an app that allows you to create your vision board on your iPhone or iPad. This is very effective.

A vision board will assist you in clarifying your goals, help you establish new habits, encourage you to take action and cause you to focus your energy on achieving your goal.

This exercise plants the seed for a life full of goals and aspirations. Once you look at things you desire and affix them in your mind, it helps the manifestation process. And children are so creative that it is great fun. Visualization is one of the greatest keys to success. Daydreaming or visualization helps children process information and explore ideas. There have been substantial studies that connect daydreaming in children with creativity, healthy social adjustment and good academic performance. A social component is associated with the visualization process, which enhances social skills and creates empathy within the child.

Seeing words on the screen of your mind is what makes the words come to life. Think about that. The visioneering process is so much easier for children in the developmental stages of their lives. It not only teaches them to be tactical thinkers, but also assists them in relaxing, exercising, showing gratitude and laughing. Visualization can help children with ADD/ADHD, which places them in a state of stress. Hyperactive and impulsive children don't know how to relax. I make hypnotherapy tapes for my ADD/ADHD clients, and the results are amazing. It helps them be calm, which then allows them to become emotionally involved in the visioneering process.

We were taught as children not to daydream, but in reality dreaming is what transforms our goals into reality and makes us better people. Unfortunately, both children and adults endure stressful situations. It could be fear of the dark, anxieties about school, bullying or ordinary child experiences.

I have a ten-year-old coaching client who experienced anxiety and fear. I made this child a hypnotherapy tape and taught him how to perform the breathing techniques. With hypnotherapy the client is given suggestions upon reaching the hypnotic state, which is the part of the session that delivers the therapeutic message. It is the technique that assists in promoting accelerated human change. Suggestion creates desired changes in behavior and encourages mental and physical well-being. There are parts of hypnosis that can be self administered, which could provide assistance in the relaxation methods to assist you in your visualization process.

Below is the child's testimonial.

Peggy has become an important person in my life because she has helped me with my anxiety. She is so amazing, and she can help me with any problem by taking three deep breaths and relaxing. She has taught me that fear (false evidence appearing real) is fake, and that helps me not to believe in fear. Recently I started a hypnotherapy tape that I listen to every night at bedtime. It makes me relax and calm down for a peaceful sleep. It also helps me with

positive thoughts for the next day. That is why I feel
Peggy is an important person in my life.
—**Dante**, ten years old—

Dreaming and visualizing assist children and adults with relaxation techniques.

- Breathing: slows down your heart rate, increases blood flow, improves concentration, reduces pain, boosts confidence and reduces anger. Whether children or adults encounter negative emotions, such as fear, worry or doubt, relating to anxiety, stress, testing, confidence boosters, and so on, learning breathing techniques will help eliminate that negative outcome. The following are two different techniques. The first one is the hypnotic relaxation technique: Take a deep breath—breathe in really deep and hold it as long as you can, then release it slowly through your mouth. Repeat it three times. This will begin the calming process. The second one is the Jacobsen technique, which is a muscle relaxation technique: Tense your arms/hands, hold five to seven seconds, then relax; next, tense your face/head, hold five to seven seconds, then relax; next, tense your chest/shoulders/ stomach, hold five to seven seconds, then relax; and, last, tense your legs/feet, hold five to seven seconds, then relax.

- Muscle relaxation for smaller children: There are multiple relaxation techniques: hypnosis, massage therapy, tai chi and yoga. Some techniques require you to use both visual imagery and body awareness. For instance, when you are striving to reduce stress, you would use an autogenic relaxation technique in which you repeat words or suggestions to relax and reduce muscle tension.

There are several ways to make this fun for children. Ask your children to think of something that smells or tastes funny and wrinkle their noses. Then have them think of something good and relax their faces. Repeat it several times.

Another way would be to have them tighten their jaws; then release and repeat. Arms, shoulders, hands and arms: have them visualize tightly squeezing an object, raise it above the head, stretching, and finally release; repeat. Stomach: have them tighten stomach muscles, release; repeat. Legs and feet: have them pretend they're scrunching their toes in the sand or picking up rocks, spread them, release; repeat.

- Exercise: this is easy because all children love to jump, run, walk, dance, swim and, most important, play! And encourage them as teens to join a gym or exercise program.
- LAUGH! Tell jokes, funny stories, make silly faces or watch cartoons. Watch a comedy together

with teens. Bring laughter into the family life. Just spend quality time listening and laughing with your children. Play with your pet. Pets are wonderful and are known to lower their owners' blood pressure and reduce stress. They bring much laughter to families. Also, laugh at each other. Do something silly to make your children laugh. You can do this from infancy through the teenage years. You could purchase a funny poster to hang in their room or choose a funny screensaver for the computer. Remember: Laughter releases happy endorphins in your brain.

When you have a heartfelt belly laugh, all parts of your being—the physiological, the psychological, the spiritual—they all vibrate in one single tune. They all vibrate in harmony.

—Osho—

- Listen to music. Choose those with encouraging lyrics and good dancing. This is powerful at all ages. As I previously mentioned, just ensure proper lyrics.
- Meditate. At bedtime, teach your children to close their eyes, picture something wonderful about the day, and breathe slowly. Have them snuggle their favorite stuffed animal in the process. Teens and adults can also meditate by thinking of something happy and positive such as a goal or

vision. Have them picture it as if it has already happened. Calmness of mind is very important and learning how to meditate will benefit them throughout the day.

I teach children to meditate just as I do with adults. With children you can incorporate the stuffed animals or favorite toy. You must educate your child on the focus of positivity. Keep them focused with concentration of happy thoughts and make them aware of the detriments to negative thoughts. Negative thoughts are unhealthy.

With your teenager or yourself, try to make quality time in the evening because the last forty-five minutes before bed are essential in the thought process. We need to incorporate these relaxation techniques as adults. Relaxation and meditation are essential to the daily routine for you or your child. Doing them together with your child, at any age, promotes good health and quality family bonding and supports creativity.

Creative imagination, auto suggestion and all self-administered stimuli which reach one's mind through the five senses is the agency of communication between that part of the mind where conscious thought takes place and that which serves as the seat of action for the subconscious mind. No thought can enter the subconscious mind without the aid of the principle of autosuggestion.

Creative imagination is the receiving set of the brain. Utilizing your senses with creative imagination helps it to become a reality. You are like a radio receiving station, whereas you can tune in to whatever you like, happiness or sadness, success or failure, optimism or fear.

> *Parents must lead by example. Don't use the cliché "Do as I say, not as I do." We are our children's first and most important role models.*
>
> **—Lee Haney—**

Let me give you an example based on similar situations. I've encountered multiple clients who are now in their twenties and experiencing negativity (that is, cutting, depression, alcohol, drugs, and the like). This resulted from visualizations displayed during the adolescent years. In some instances the parents' interests helped establish thoughts within the child. For example, if a parent's interests contained images of skulls, horror movies or gothic items, then the child may very well grow up to have similar interests. I've seen such interests cause them to love video games that involved extreme violence. That type of violence can lead to criminal behavior. The same holds true for a parent with alcoholic tendencies. Anything that contains negativity, such as those listed, can cause addictions, depression or cutting.

I just mentioned the topic of cutting. It is a negative tendency of children who internalize their emotions. They do not know how to release and therefore dwell on negatives. Not understanding how to release creates confusion, anger, disappointment, and fears within them. They release their negative emotions by cutting parts of their bodies with a sharp instrument, such as a knife, scissors, pins or needles.

Cutting is a major problem in today's society. I see it in children as young as ten. I've coached children and teens who have cut themselves because of anger issues but also because of disappointment in their physical appearance. When parents tell their children repeatedly that they are concerned about their weight, the children may internalize, feel as if they are fat and ugly and then begin to cut their bodies.

This does not happen with everyone. In documented cases two children have come from the same alcoholic and abusive parent; one grew up to be just like the parent while the other learned from it and grew up to have a successful and happy life with no tendencies. But why would anyone want to risk the outcome? Plant good seeds and be a positive role model.

Remember the power of visualization. It is truly part of the creative process.

Now. . .what do they truly desire?
Let's help them reveal it.

Chapter 3

What Do Your Children Desire, And How Can You Help Them Get There?

Be the change that you want to see in the world.
—Mohandas Gandhi—

After a screen test the memo from the director read, "Can't act. Can't sing. Slightly bald. Can dance a little."
—Fred Astaire—

Fired after his first performance at the Grand Ole Opry and told by his manager, "You ain't going nowhere, son. You ought to go back to driving a truck."
—**Elvis Presley**—

W hat does your child truly desire?

I was sitting in my office and looked up. There she was—Emily. Such a beautiful girl, but it was evident she was withdrawn, depressed, unorganized, and extremely negative. How could someone eighteen years of age with such beauty be so down on life? Emily was cutting herself, a significant problem in children that age. She didn't want to go to college and was currently seeking psychiatric therapy and taking medications for major depression, anxiety, and attention deficit disorder.

Emily and I worked together for months implementing tools and techniques to assist her with her anxiety and building her self-esteem. At the end of our time together she was taken off her medication; she attends college and is very happy. She would never cut herself now, and I am proud of her accomplishments. She is also proud of her accomplishments and discusses it openly. She actually offered to be interviewed on my radio show.

On my website www.lifecoachingandbeyond.com go to the tab marked "Podcasts" and feel free to listen to my radio interview with Emily.

Below is Emily's testimonial as to how life coaching made a significant difference in her life.

When I was around fourteen my mom started to notice I wasn't the happy little girl I used to be. I was impulsive, unorganized, unfocused, and I saw myself in a negative light. I started psychiatric treatment not long after this observation and was diagnosed with several disorders: major depression, anxiety and attention deficit being the main ones. I was prescribed a few different medications and was on them for about three years. But I had started to realize the medications were just masking my problems, and I needed a way to face them. Life coaching with Peggy was exactly what I was looking for. In our sessions we would work on techniques for raising my self-esteem, how to turn every situation positive, facing my fears, focusing, and much more. She gave me tools I will be able to use for the rest of my life. In the beginning of my journey I felt hopeless. I felt like I wasn't worth being helped. After I started life coaching, I soon realized I am worth being helped. EVERYONE is. Remember that there is always help available, and you can change how you are living your life at any point in time. Believe in yourself and your potential. I believe in you!
—**Emily**, age eighteen—

What was Emily's desire?

To be what she considered to be normal. But Emily is and always has been normal. She just became side tracked. But why? Well, it's what we previously discussed. Her difficulties began during the modeling period, and when she moved into the socialization period she had experienced bullying and peer pressure in school. This was the beginning of her depression and cutting. The depression brought on a lack of focus and an inability to be organized. Emily needed to learn how to have calmness of mind.

Calmness of mind is imperative in providing clarity and focus. You as a parent need that same calmness in order to assist your child.

James Allen's *As a Man Thinketh* explains calmness of mind in his "Serenity" chapter.

> Calmness of mind is one of the beautiful jewels of wisdom. It is the result of long and patient effort in self-control. Its presence is an indication of ripened experience and of a more than ordinary knowledge of the laws and operations of thought.

He later adds:

> The strong, calm man is always loved and revered. He is like a shade-giving tree in a thirsty land, or a sheltering rock in a storm.

Allen explains:

That exquisite poise of character which we call serenity is the last lesson of culture; it is the flowering of life, the fruitage of the soul. It is precious as wisdom, more to be desired than gold—yea, than even fine gold.

And his ending thoughts are powerful:

Keep your hand firmly upon the helm of thought. In the barque of your soul reclines the commanding Master; He does but sleep; wake Him. Self-control is strength; Right Thought is mastery; Calmness is power. Say unto your heart, "Peace be still!"

We need to instill calmness of mind in our children. I've spoken with many teachers who agree that calmness of mind creates focus in children. A friend of mine, *Melissa Mulhollan,* has been a high school English teacher at a comprehensive vocational-technical school. This is a school that brings students in for their shop experience and provides their academic coursework all in the same building.

In an in-depth conversation with her she explained that so many of the students appeared to have lost their desire to learn. "Most educators will agree that the educational system itself needs to change and improve.

Much of the materials we offer and the manner in which we do so cannot hold the interest of some of the brightest students as we compete with television, video games and the internet."

She went on to discuss her thoughts on what her students were feeling. "It was not that these kids didn't care; it wasn't that they couldn't learn the materials—they simply didn't **BELIEVE** *they could do it. The key then was not how creative I was in delivering my lessons or providing the materials to them. It was getting these kids to understand they deserved to learn, they could learn,* and they needed to have goals and aspire to make them all come true.

"I began a haphazard approach to delivering these concepts to my classes. I noticed many of my students perking up and taking notice of what I was saying. I understood I may not reach all of them as I attempted to get them to believe in themselves; but I knew with all my heart I would be able to reach many more with this type of approach. I also realized that the students who during high school would fail to utilize the information and techniques I was now implementing might end up using them futuristically. I hoped the students would benefit now with what I was doing with them as well as later on when they were out in the real world. I knew what I was doing was right but wasn't certain I knew the best way to help them.

One morning, as I was getting ready for work, I heard an ad on our most popular local radio station about a life-coaching business coming to DuBois. The ad described what a life coach could do for people, from dealing with depression, anxiety and weight loss to helping entrepreneurs with their business endeavors. It was all about taking a positive approach toward setting goals. I jumped up and grabbed a pen and paper and jotted down the name "Life Coaching and Beyond, Peggy Caruso" followed by her phone number. I was so excited that I might have found a trained professional who could help me with my new approach to teaching.

"I called Peggy that morning. When we spoke I told her what I had been doing with my students. Everything she told me was exactly what I had been trying to do with them. I asked her if she would come in and speak with one of my groups of seniors."

She continually reinforces the positive impact her students have on goal setting. Our approach to apply the principles I use in coaching has been very effective. She said, "As I read Peggy's book, completed her workbook, continued talking with her and am now taking a life-coaching course from her, I have become the teacher I have longed to become and so much more. The first group of students I taught using the knowledge and tools provided to me from Peggy were extremely successful.

"Not only did I develop an incredible rapport with these students, but fifty-nine percent of them were proficient or advanced on our Keystone exams in literature. That was an eleven percent increase from the previous year; we are comparing my students who earned that percentage their sophomore year to the students who took it the previous year as juniors.

"I also know it is not only what I have learned and done with my students, but also making those changes within myself. You cannot be a fraud without children or teens knowing it. I had to implement these changes in my own life and am a better person because of it. I still have a lot to learn, and it is truly a process, but it has been more than worth it. I will continue to use what I learn from Peggy and will continue learning how to be the best person and teacher I can be. I will be that lifelong learner, and I will continue to hone those skills for the rest of my life. Life coaching has saved my life and has made a difference in the lives of my students. I am so happy and grateful."

A burning desire to succeed makes you fully committed; that is why most people fail to achieve their goals. My perception of what I have presented shows that the most creative dreamers have the determination and commitment to understand your internal belief is the power to attain success.

I speak often of a story about the Greek warriors. In history the ancient Greek warriors were both feared and respected by their enemies for their reputation of unsurpassed bravery and commitment to victory. Once the warriors arrived on the enemy's shore, the commanders ordered them to "burn the boats." With no boats to retreat to, the army had to survive. As the soldiers watched the boats burn, they realized there was no turning back, no surrendering. The same stands true in your own life and where you have arrived. That is why I love that story; you have no excuses for failure. You must win or perish. I have used that process to attain victory in my own life. It is a huge leap of faith!

Think of all the missed opportunities in your life because you didn't burn the boats.

Remove those obstacles and excuses;
Storm the shore with a successful attitude;
Let your fear and regret burn with the boat;
Leave it at the bottom of the water.

You will be victorious! Imagine the psychological impact on the soldiers when they realized there was no turning back. It removed from their minds any notion of retreat or surrender. In your scenario you will not battle on the shore, but in your mind. Also remember that temporary defeat states,

Every failure brings with it the seed of equivalent success.

Relate that story to your child. Teaching them to burn the boats builds inner strength and helps them realize nothing is impossible.

Many of my teenage clients perform a symbolic exercise that imprints gratitude and faith. The end result helps them see their true desire and know they have the strength to persevere.

When children are negative, I encourage them to make a list of everything they are negative about. We then take a piece of paper and write the complete opposite, that is, what is positive. On completion I ask them to burn the negative list. They then focus on the positive list and after a while cannot remember the negatives.

It takes approximately thirty days for change to take place in the subconscious mind. Therefore, repetition and positive affirmations are imperative. Knowing their desire is what assists in goal setting—yes, goal setting for children. People tend to believe goal setting is only for adults; however, children who set goals are far more likely to become successful as adults.

Your child may have only small desires but understand you need only one intense desire to accomplish your goals. Concentrate on one definite object, one idea at a time, and become absorbed. Do not confuse desire with imagination.

> Imagination is the dream…the vision,
> but desire is the internal will,
> the ongoing obsession;
> so concentrate, focus, feel it
> and believe it.

They all work simultaneously. Once you understand the burning desire, you will be excited to realize you can produce anything you want, be anything you want and accomplish anything you set out to do if you hold that desire steady with purpose. Conscious desire may not deliver, but the desire that is impressed upon the subconscious will surely deliver. Once you impress upon it you have opened the door of opportunity which is never closed.

Remember there are no limits, no law
of limitation, unless you impress upon them.
Aim high! Whatever price you
set upon yourself, life will give.
Aim for the moon, but if you miss
you will surely hit a star.
When you reveal your desire,
it creates an internal enthusiasm;
it motivates you to move forward.
Teach your child:
Begin at once...see it, feel it,
become excited then apply faith.

Chapter 4

What Happens To Your Child When Intuition And Faith Are Applied?

Children are the hands by which we take hold of heaven.

—Henry Ward Beecher—

When he was a boy his teacher told him he was too stupid to learn anything. He was fired from his first two jobs for not being productive enough.

—Thomas Edison—

Rejected by a recording company, they were told, "We don't like your sound, and guitar music is on its way out."

—The Beatles—

The child came to me during the modeling period with no friends, negative and annoyed with life. We applied many tools and techniques aimed in a positive direction; implementing the belief theory accelerated the changes.

The child had no religious beliefs so I helped him believe in energy. While progressing, the child spoke of a higher being and accepted the thought of heaven. By implementing this belief system it was easy to get the child to be grateful for things. He became less annoyed and attracted new friends.

When children don't believe in a higher power it affects their ability to be grateful. When they have a belief system it makes them feel as though they are held accountable to someone other than the parents and at a higher level. Children and teens experience many ups and downs with their parents, and many go through a stage of intolerance, resentment or lack of respect. Believing that someone else makes you accountable for your actions helps accelerate the progression. Once I could get the child to believe in a power for good, I could then work on positivity and gratitude.

In a similar coaching setting I had a young girl who talked about the power of positivity through the process. At first she didn't want to apply it because of the difficulty in believing someone without proof. But once she noticed some positive changes with applying the program she began to think in a different way. I encouraged her to do her own due diligence. The child validated what I was teaching by going on the Internet and researching positivity.

"The method that worked the best for me," she said, "was that every time I thought something negative I had to reverse the entire thought and think something positive. It was extremely hard for me at first especially when I was mad at my brother or sister or mom. It got a lot easier for me whenever I became more positive. My life coach had been telling me to say to myself what I was happy and grateful for every single morning before I got up. But I never did it. One day I went onto the Internet and searched how to become more positive. My negativity was overpowering my life; I was always upset and grumpy and would hide out in my bedroom. My family started calling it my cave.

"On the Internet I read that to reverse any negative thought I needed to think something positive. For example, when I found out the guy I liked actually liked someone else I was really upset. The old negative me would have been crying and eating any sugar I could find. Instead I said, 'I am very happy it is somebody who is kind and caring and super positive' rather than, 'I hate my life and have no friends' as the old me would have said.

"Another trick I learned was to create a happy wall. Well, that was what I called it. Every night I had to come up with something positive that happened to me. I would write it down on a post-it note and stick it on my wall. Every time I was feeling lonely I would go to my wall and read every single sticky note.

"I had practiced these tricks over a weekend while I was visiting with my dad in Pittsburgh. My mom had already seen a huge difference in me the weekend before. Of course I stuck to it longer than just a weekend. The key to positivity though was to have motivation. I didn't want to be "that girl" anymore. I was always in the back of class doing my work, and on weekends I would read rather than going on Facebook or Instagram like the rest of my friends. When I became more positive I accomplished what I never thought possible: I became popular. Not the mean kind, but the kind of popular everyone wanted to hang out with because I was positive and caring. I have always been a great friend, but people began hanging out with me when I became happier."

Learning positivity and gratitude helped prevent depression and cutting. It helped her see the benefit of teaching others the same and allowed her to be a friend to those in need. She also said, "When your children or friends or cousins are depressed and cutting or destroying their lives or just being negative, let them know you are there for them."

Renee, 12 years old

Working daily with children it is evident the impact a belief system makes. Behavior modification occurs much faster in those who believe in a higher power. Those who have no belief have nothing to fear and therefore no one to disappoint. They have a "who cares" attitude. Also, with no belief system there is minimal room for gratitude.

It appears that when they don't believe in a higher power they have minimal belief in their capabilities. I coached several teenage girls who had no faith in their abilities and no religious beliefs. They were unable to pass tests, communicate with strangers or even understand the steps one would take to apply for employment. After constant repetition of affirmations, incorporating gratitude, and boosting self-esteem we began to see results. Jack Canfield continually teaches a "mirror exercise" which assists in helping those with low self-esteem. He recommends you stand naked in front of a mirror every night and repeatedly say all the things you love about yourself and what you are grateful for. You must learn how to love yourself for what and who you are before you can portray any positivity. You can't love the inside until you love the outside, and likewise you can't love the outside until you love the inside.

Thoughts, mixed with emotion and faith, translate themselves into their physical equivalent or counterpart. In my research I have found that science demonstrates the possibility to accomplish good; but distrust of your abilities to reach your desired goal will create reservation within you and result in failure.

Once you understand this power is the universal mind and not circumstances or environment, you will surely cause your abilities to surface. There are multiple beliefs throughout the world; however, few will deny the intelligence that governs this universe. When reading the writings of another, what matters most to me is that whether referenced as God, universal mind, supreme intelligence, nature, etc., it is a force for good. All of our minds are part of this "force for good" just as the sun's rays are part of the sun. We must all be harmonious to attract it for power, and it's insufficient unless you repetitively practice it. Bob Proctor speaks of the seven laws are said to govern the universe and below is how he explains it:

- Law of perpetual transmutation—energy flows to and through us. An ocean of motion. Energy moves into physical form, and it can't be created or destroyed. Thought energy builds ideas then takes the energy and impresses it into the subconscious mind. It then sets up emotion, which, in turn, produces action. This is part of the creative process. To live in harmony with this law, always be aware, and sometimes beware of your thoughts and feelings. If they are anything but pleasing, do whatever you can to make them positive.

- Law of relativity—nothing is big or small, fast or slow, good or bad, until you relate it to something else. Everything just is. All laws must be in harmony with each other. Don't relate your results to another's success. Relate it to what you truly desire. To live in harmony with this law heighten your self-esteem and increase the image you hold of yourself. You will then become aware of how special you are in the light of truth.

- Law of vibration—conscious awareness that your vibration is in feeling; therefore, your mind is movement and attraction is a result of the vibration you're in. All communication is based on the law of vibration. This is huge in sales. Everything in the universe vibrates; nothing rests. Action and attraction! Use it to pick up another's vibration (intuition). Do not allow another's negative energy to affect your vibration. When you concentrate, your thoughts get stronger. They are cosmic waves of energy that penetrate time and space. Your thought controls the vibration your physical body is in. Your brain is your vibration switching station. You think with your brain. Use it to improve your life. When you say you're thinking you are choosing to activate certain brain cells. They, in turn, affect your central nervous system, and you move in to whatever vibration those particular cells govern. The law of attraction begins to deliver what you are thinking about. Brain cells are where you store your mental images. To live in harmony with this law choose happy pictures. If you're not feeling good, become aware of what you are thinking, and then improve it.

- Law of rhythm—everything is moving up and down, to and from, high and low, swinging back and forth. Every action has a reaction—the rising and setting of the sun, the coming and going of the seasons, the flowing in and out of the tides. The rhythmic swing of consciousness and unconsciousness. Your low feelings are what permit you to feel the high feelings. Life will always have its highs and lows. Reason gives us the ability to choose our thoughts—that is, free will. Everyone experiences low points, but you have the free will to focus on the high points. President Nixon said upon resigning, *"It's only by experiencing the depths of the valley that you will enjoy the magnificence of the mountain.," President Nixon*. To live in harmony with this law think of the good times coming. Even if you are on a down swing, don't feel bad; know that, by law, the swing will change, and things can only get better. Embrace this law.

- Law of polarity, or opposites—you can't have an in without an out, an up without a down, a front without a back, an inside without an outside, dark without light. Not only does everything have an opposite, but also an equal and opposite. If something is bad in your life, something is also good. Focus on the positive. If it's only a little bad, when you work your way around it to the other side, it's only a little good. Remember everything just is. Don't react; just respond and keep on going. To me, this is the best law because you realize every bad has a good. To live in harmony with this law, look for the good in people and when you find it tell the person.

- Law of cause and effect—every cause has an effect, and every effect has a cause. *"There is no such thing as chance or luck," Ralph Waldo Emerson.* As you sow so shall you reap. Concentrate on the cause (material income, health, respect, and so on) and the effect will take care of itself. Law of psychological reciprocity—you get back what you give is a law within this law. When you put a positive out you will get a positive back, but rarely right away. But when you put a negative out you'll get one right back. When someone gives you a positive give them one right back, and when someone gives you a negative step aside and let it keep on going. Bob Proctor compares it metaphorically to martial arts: Karate is where you hit me, and I hit you; you kick me, and I kick you. Judo is where you take the strength of another person's shot and put them down with it. You win the battle, but lose the war. Aikido is when someone takes a shot at you; you duck and let it keep on going. This continues until they've worn themselves out. You're fresh and can lead them to where you want them to go. When you compliment they'll send good vibrations back;

but when you yell at someone and treat them improperly they'll yell back. To live in harmony with this law never worry about what you are going to receive; just concentrate on what you can give. Remember that energy returns to its source of origination.

- Law of gender—misunderstanding this law tends to cause people to feel as though they failed. All things are manifested as masculine and feminine. This governs creation and completes the seven subsidiary laws. Everything is male and female and is required for existence. All seeds have an incubation period before they manifest. Ideas are spiritual seeds. When you envision a dream or goal in your mind a definite period of time must elapse before it's manifested in physical form. All ideas move into form and on an intellectual level as soon as you think about them. As you turn them over to your emotional mind they manifest physically. You don't know how long it will take in the gestation period. To live in harmony with this law plant good seeds.

When you come to the edge of all the light you have and are about to step off into the darkness of the unknown, faith is knowing one of two things will happen. There will be something solid to stand on, or you will be taught how to fly.

—Patrick Overton—

What is your sixth sense or intuition, and how is it related to faith?

Intuition is in close comparison to faith, which denotes a certainty or unwavering knowing, transcending reason and logic. It consists of objective facts and subjective human knowledge. Intuition is the communication link between the outer world and the unconscious inner world.

It is that portion of information that lies beyond the subconscious mind, which has been referred to as the creative imagination. It has also been referred to as the receiving set through which ideas, plans, and thoughts flash into the mind. The flashes are sometimes called hunches or inspirations.

In simplest terms, intuition is the mental process of acquiring information and knowledge directly into the mind without the use of reasoning, sensing or even memory.

Nearly all great leaders, such as Napoleon, Bismark, Joan of Arc, Jesus Christ, Buddha, Confucius, and Mohammed understood, and probably made use of, the sixth sense almost continuously. Henry Ford and Thomas Edison undoubtedly understood the sixth sense and made practical use of it.

The sixth sense is a mixture of mental and spiritual: all groups (for example, psychiatrists, psychologists, physicians and the churches) use the one universal power resident in the subconscious mind. It is psychic, or paranormality, parapsychology, or spirituality. Even though each may claim the healings are due to their own particular theory, the process of all healing is a definite, positive, mental attitude, namely, faith. With variances in belief of theory or method, the one method of healing unanimously agreed upon is faith.

Regardless of which theory is your own belief, you can rest assured faith brings results. We all know of the famous saying, "The doctor dresses the wound, but God heals it." So, you see, it's not the psychologist, psychiatrist, family practitioner, or religious leader that heals the patient. The modern mental therapeutic procedure is based upon the truth that the infinite intelligence and power of your subconscious mind respond according to faith. I recently read some corresponding literature from multiple sources that portrayed this same message: "Imagine the ending result of your desire and feel its reality; then the infinite intelligence wil respond to your request." This contains the meaning of "Believe you have received, and you shall receive." This is what the modern mental scientist does when he practices prayer therapy.

Your sixth sense guides you to keep you out of harm's way by providing a warning. Intuition means inner sight, inner consciousness, and inner knowledge. It is defined as immediate mental apprehension without reasoning, immediate insight. It fills the gap and attempts to assist you in attaining your desired results. Everyone has this psychic power, but very few learn how to develop it.

How do you develop intuition?

You need to remove the mental blocks and enhance sensitivity to the part of your inner mind. You need to learn to communicate with your inner mind by involving your feelings and learning how to distinguish genuine feelings of the heart from emotional reactions from your subconscious mind.

- Hypnosis
- Meditation
- Thinking positive
- Letting go
- Never expecting
- Believing in your first impressions
- Staying happy

What are some ways in which your children might develop intuition?

- Choices: Teach them when choosing between two toys in a store. Choose the one that gives them the strongest feeling. Teach them what an internal feeling means. For example: when a stranger attempts to speak to them and they are shy it is their inner feeling regarding safety. Utilize the same strategy for teens substituting something for the toys. Teach them choices in relationships.
- People's thoughts and emotions: If you touch on a subject and your children share with you that they had the same thought let them know it is a form of intuition. Children are especially sensitive in absorbing other people's energy. When they

become difficult it could possibly be the result of absorbing negative energy from others. They might even do so if you are stressed and worried your children will absorb the negativity. The same holds true for your teen.

• Play intuitive games: Guessing colors, shapes, "who's on the phone" game. Something corresponding for your teen.

Now it's time to discover the hidden causes of negativity.

Chapter 5

Divorce, Separation, Stepchildren, Bullying… Help!

An aware parent loves all children he or she interacts with—for you are a caretaker for those moments in time.

—Doc Childre—

Enduring a rough and abusive childhood she faced numerous setbacks including being fired from her first job because she was unfit for TV.

—Oprah Winfrey—

She was broke, severely depressed, divorced and a single mother while attending school and attempting to write her first novel.

—J. K. Rowling—

*T*here she was, a beautiful young girl with a face showing anger and a heart filled with sadness. No self esteem, withdrawn, no friends, poor academic performance, expressing outbursts of anger and a complete lack of empathy toward people and animals. She was beginning to experience uncontrolled anger, which was leading toward problems involving law enforcement. The father of the child relinquished his parental rights, and hope was diminishing. The mother contacted me and asked me to help so I began by coaching the child. Working with the mother, she was home-schooled for the remainder of the school year. Daily teachings needed to be applied. The first item on my agenda was to teach the child about gratitude. To have a child with no self esteem and no empathy toward others means that the child does not know how to be grateful for anything or anyone. She internalized her negative emotions, which caused her to be withdrawn; so teaching her how to replace negatives with positives was the next step.

It takes a minimum of thirty days for change to take place in the subconscious mind; therefore, my plan would consist of thirty uninterrupted days. Once a child begins to alter their way of thinking and believing in who they are, they can then start to visualize dreams and goals. She had no faith; therefore, I applied the teaching that you must believe in a higher power, that is, a power for good.

While occupying her mind with positivity and eliminating the worry of the school system and bullying, I was then able to create a visionary process that would include the value of friendship. After all, who can attract friends if they are continually angry and negative?

I then performed a discover-your-skill-set exercise to determine her strengths, weaknesses, passion and talents. In doing this we discovered she was extremely artistic so I did some research. I like to help children become a "kidpreneur" so this was easy for me. I found a program that teaches children how to become cartoonists, so I purchased it and began to work with her. Buying the right supplies and promoting practice made it a successful endeavor. I then taught entrepreneurial skills so she could learn to build her own business.

At this point a decision needed to be made regarding her education, so she was enrolled in a private school for the next year. The foundation had been built, which allowed her to make confident decisions. I strive to reinforce the principals of my teaching; at times we experience negativity, but turning it around has become much easier.

As in this case, multiple problems stemmed from abuse, neglect, bullying, and abandonment. What are some of the causes?

Divorce/separation

Divorce has a major impact on your child(ren). The factoring component is age. I have multiple clients ranging from age nine to twenty-three, and verifiably within all was the age factor. Those who came from families where divorce occurred before the age of five had little or no recollection and no major impact. But the ones who experienced it later in life expressed opinions. The fact that adolescents have a more difficult time with divorce is partly due to developmental changes within the child.

Some of the parents have brought their children to me since they went through a divorce. Reports from the parents and teachers have included problem behavior, social issues, psychological distress, and poor academic performance. In some cases the family's economic circumstances have changed as well.

Single parenting is also an issue and has a major impact on the child. Not only does the child experience emotional distress, but divorce has an impact on the parent's resources, attitudes, and socialization goals.

In the case of frequent fighting there was approval. It was a relief to have the verbal, and in some cases, physical abuse eliminated. There are many instances where husband and wife stay together because of fear of how divorce will impact the child; but if there is no attempt to repair the marriage and the arguing is continual, then the impact on the child remains negative.

In some cases the child may not have been exposed to abuse or argumentative situations, therefore causing negative and bitter emotions regarding divorce. In that instance confusion lies within the mind of the child. It is evident that blame causes negativity within the child. That negativity creates emotion they internalize and in turn causes emotional destruction.

If you are experiencing divorce, pay special attention to differences in their self-image, behavior and socialization. In general, people tend to believe marital dissolution can create considerable turmoil; but some people believe divorce has been a benefit to the child. You need to take into consideration all of the factors leading up to the divorce or separation. Again, there are children who speak to me about the relief of eliminating negativity within the household.

Communication is an area I speak of quite frequently. It is key in all relationships. Therefore, talk to your children about the feelings, both positive and negative, so they can comprehend the impact it will have on their lives going forward.

The best advice I can give is that you and your spouse need to communicate in a positive way for the sake of the outcome of your child's behavior. Many parents say they can get along better being apart than together.

Living with stepparents/brothers/sisters

While coaching children and teenagers I have recognized the impact it has had on those who live with step-parents and step-brothers/sisters. Very few cases I have come in contact with are healthy. Jealousy, bitterness and the misconception of love and loyalty in children's minds leave them with a sense of distrust of the parent. This is not applicable to all situations. I mention it so that if you are exposing your children to a living environment that consists of a step-parent/brother/sister you can study their behavioral patterns to analyze if they are feeling that way. In some instances love and trust exist between the families. This book is to educate you on reasons why your child may be internalizing negative emotions.

Many factors relate to these types of living arrangements, and areas of discussion in this book do not apply to everyone. I am viewing it from the area of complication. The children I coach normally experience the downside of divorce and then a new relationship.

If you don't effectively communicate with your children, they tend to feel as though they are the cause. You must ensure they realize the reason(s) you have decided to separate or divorce and then reinforce the love you both feel toward your children.

When one or both of the divorced parents decide to become involved in a new relationship multiple factors can lead to behavioral issues. Jealousy of the other parent being in a new relationship brings negative emotions and then perhaps neglect. The parent who watches this new relationship develop has many emotions: fear of being alone; fear of the new person winning over his/her child; fear of losing primary custody; fear of rejection. Fears are crippling and can cause worry, doubt, stress and anxiety.

Often the parent tries to win the trust of the stepchild, and in doing so his or her own child feels neglect. It is a tough situation because all parties experience many emotions.

You must make yourself aware of how the stepchildren are feeling as well. Their own parents may at times play against each other to please the child. There is also the pressure of a new parent.

Studies show that one-third of Americans are stepparents, stepchildren, stepsiblings, or some other member of a stepfamily. The number of children living with both biological parents has declined, and the number of children living in a stepfamily has increased. It is important to allow time to adjust to any situation.

Many research studies have examined the effects of remarriage on children. Some studies have shown that many children find the remarriage of a parent more stressful than the actual divorce. Some problems include lack of self-esteem, stress, anxiety, behavioral issues, attitudes, social distress, and poor academic achievement. Again, this doesn't apply to every situation. According to many documented cases stepchildren may do better than when they were with the biological parents.

If you choose to have more children with your new partner, realize the impact a new baby will have on everyone involved. You will definitely need time to adjust time. A new mother in an old family (first baby for the mother, but not the father) will have to cope with the added stress of new parenthood as well as additional pressures. New mothers experience jealousy from knowing he has already been through this with another woman and resentment that he spends time with his other children.

An old dad in a new family can also be difficult. He may worry about the feelings of his other children and may feel drawn to his new family and withdraw from his old. Relationships may also become complicated with the ex-spouse and grandparents.

Many issues stem from the pressures of divorce. The financial stress plays a vital role as well as balancing career and family obligations. In many instances, the families have gone from a two-parent household, with both parents sharing the domestic obligations, to that of the primary caregiver being solely responsible. This affects moods and attitudes and results in anger and coping capabilities.

Try to remember that, regardless of family structure, positive spousal relations enhance the child's ability to adapt to the new situation. The younger the child, the easier it is for making positive behavioral changes because consistent routines accelerate the outcome.

I have touched on multiple areas that cause conflict and emotional distress and left out some. The scenarios are endless; therefore, it is imperative that you study changes in your child's behavioral patterns. Divorce is difficult for everyone, and the parent(s) tend to get caught up in their own emotional, physical and financial issues. This leads to an unintentional bypass of the child.

I believe in almost all cases it is unintentional. So many added pressures are on every level. It would be wise to allow your child to speak to a professional who can study the behavior and know exactly what to look for and what preventive measures can be taken.

Bullying

Here is a story from a client (*Adam*, twenty-three years old):

When I was young, I was happy, energetic, and just loved being alive. Then my life changed, more specifically, first grade happened. I was depressed and withdrawn and hated my existence to the extent that one night I attempted suicide. Why the sudden change? What happened? Bullying. Bullying is an area I know quite well. This is one of the major issues that have affected my childhood, teens, and early adulthood. I did not want someone else to shoulder my burden, so I treated my situation akin to a disease. I tried to keep up an "I'm fine" facade around my parents because I didn't want them to worry. A feeling of powerlessness was the major factor contributing to all my childhood hardships. Peggy aims to show you, the parent, what I consider the two major aspects to counteracting bullying: empowerment and identification. Empowering your children is vital to helping them safeguard against negative encounters and identifying "trouble spots" that they may be hiding from you.

Bullying is very prevalent and problematic in today's society. It shows up in several forms:

- Physical bullying—includes hitting, kicking, tripping, pushing, and damaging property.
- Verbal bullying—includes teasing, name calling, and verbal abuse.
- Covert bullying—includes lying, rumors, negative gestures, humiliation, damaging someone's reputation, or encouraging others to exclude someone socially. This is more difficult to recognize and prove because it is done behind the person's back.
- Cyber bullying—includes behaviors listed above (excluding physical) using digital technologies. It is harassing others via mobile phone or computer. It can be done privately or publicly.

Bullying at any level causes the victim to have low self-esteem, physical, social or emotional health issues, depression, academic difficulties, loneliness, anxiety, suicidal ideation, or the like. The impact is severe and life altering. Coaching clients who are in their early twenties are still impacted from bullying that occurred in middle and high school. The students that perform the bullying acts are more likely to be aggressive, insecure, have poor social skills and definitely lack empathy toward others. Without proper attention the student who is the bully has a tendency to experience aggression in later years; it can also lead to violence and criminality in life.

I coached a young girl who was severely bullied in school. This caused her to become very withdrawn and angry. With no knowledge of how to release that anger or emotion, she began to take it out on animals and other people. It was a long process to apply the previous principles listed in the book, but the reward was that she learned compassion. She originally had no empathy, which can lead to criminality. The constant repetition of faith, gratitude, journaling and the visioneering process combined with discovering skills and utilizing focusing techniques allowed us to reprogram her subconscious mind and modify behavioral patterns.

Listed below are a few signs to look for when you think your child might be a victim of bullying:

- Change in sleep patterns
- Change in eating patterns
- Mood swings, including sadness and anger
- Continually complaining of being ill and not wanting to attend school
- Withdrawn
- Silent and wanting to spend time alone
- Lack of friends
- Insecure
- Behavior issues

Physical signs include:

- Bruises, cuts and scratches
- Damaging property or clothing
- Missing property or clothing

School signs include:

- Continual absence
- Fear of walking to school
- Changes route to school
- Failing grades

To determine if your children are victims of bullying, study behavior patterns, listen to them and, if you feel they have experienced it, talk to them calmly. Let them know you care, understand and can help. If you are sure they are, call the school then seek professional counseling. Many trained professionals deal with this on a daily basis.

Social media
Technology, TV, video games, and the like

Social media can play a negative role in children because of a lack of communication, resulting in their internalizing their emotions. When children internalize and don't release their emotions they can implode and turn to cutting, especially if they feel sad and angry. They may feel as if they are unworthy of love.

Another detriment to social media with children is when they encounter pornography on the Internet. You can have the most focused, well-behaved child, but curiosity sometimes takes precedence. This book is intended to help parents understand the stages of a child's life and the measures we can take to ensure safety, focus and a healthy lifestyle. But children must make mistakes so they can grow and learn lessons. It is normal for your child to be curious, but we must educate ourselves concerning Internet safety.

The scariest part of curiosity about pornography is that some of the social chat rooms are linked to international pornography rings. Several clients in the modeling period (ages seven to fourteen) encountered those types of chat rooms. These clients resulted from the social networking site, KIK. While working with the Pennsylvania State Police, these particular cases led to their being "friended" by someone in a porn ring; that in turn led them out of that chat room into one of danger. Even though a parent does due diligence, a site that looks safe may not be.

Here is a list of some of the dangerous sites. Keep in mind, though, that they will be outdated very soon and you will need to research new ones.

- Creepy—This is a site that uses a Twitter or Facebook ID to track someone's every move and find their exact location. It allows access to photos and pulls sensitive geotag location data, allowing them to pinpoint where the photo was taken.

- Ask.fm—This is a site associated with instances of cyber bullying in teens and a series of bullying-related suicides.
- Vine
- Snap chat—This is extremely popular and is widely known as the sexting app. It allows users to take photos, record videos, add text and drawings and send them to a controlled list of followers. The followers can only view the photos for a short period of time, after which Snap chat supposedly destroys them. But many users get around this "self-destructing" feature by taking screen shots of the photos. This app has been associated with numerous sexting cases among teens and have led to harassment.
- KIK - This is the app I researched extensively. It is an instant messenger service designed for use on smartphones and is widely associated with sexting.
- Pheed

It is important for you to discuss these apps openly and advise your children of the risks. I encourage you to utilize the parental control settings whereby you can block certain types of activity.

As I previously stated, the Internet is an amazing tool that, with the proper monitoring, can be very useful for your family. You can't stop technology; therefore, we need to understand and take precautionary measures. With many children being more technologically advanced than some parents, we need to preserve their moral innocence and ensure they are not putting themselves at risk by exposing sensitive information via instant messaging or e-mail. Various monitoring tools can be installed on your computer. They serve a good purpose. But we parents need to understand the threats, configure the software according to our desire and check the log-in file.

The same concerns hold true for the monitoring systems. New ones are presented often so please continually research the Internet to find the best and latest technology. The following is a list of a few current monitoring systems.

- Web Watcher—In the top pick reviews this one is rated as the best monitoring and filtering software available. It allows you to monitor your child or employee's computer from the web so you don't have to keep checking from the computer you are monitoring. Its interface is easy to use.
- Spy Agent—This has the ability to monitor what is happening on the computer and comes with a basic set of filtering tools. The tools allow you to block certain keywords or websites as well as applications based on ports.
- Content Protect— It is rated highly for filtering. It does a great job of blocking and, with its automatic override feature, allows you to unblock a site that was unintentionally blocked. It allows you to configure separate settings for each user profile so you can tailor the level of restriction

to the particular users of the computer. It has the ability to block out a user from accessing the entire Internet, instant messaging applications, newsgroups, or even peer-to-peer software.

- SpectorPro
- Eblaster
- Cyber sitter
- Net Nanny—This is not invisible, which means it shows messages to the user that he or she is committing a violation; so it should not be used if invisible monitoring and blocking are your intention. Net Nanny's real strength is the fact that it is one of the few parental control software programs that allows you to view the list of websites being blocked. It also offers a white list, which is a great way for parents to allow access to certain websites they approve of, ensuring that those sites are never blocked inadvertently. It will block pornography, do time management, mask profanity, monitor social media and send alerts and reports.
- Snoop Stick—This is a USB flash-drive type device that allows you to monitor what your kids are doing on the Internet. You can monitor them live, in real time, from anywhere in the world. It allows you to update the parental control settings of your remote computer automatically. For example, if your children are off from school, you can update the configuration to allow them access

for one hour and see remotely what they are doing during that hour.

I presently coach individuals from ages nine to twenty-five so I can ensure that social media is vital in the emotional role of a child. It can lead to difficulties as they reach maturity.

Take what you've built so far, motivate them. . . then teach them how to persist.

Chapter 6

Show Your Child
How To Persist

Children are likely to live up to what you believe in them.

—Lady Bird Johnson—

Before joining the NBA he was just an ordinary person, so ordinary he was cut from his high school basketball team due to his "lack of skill." He said, "I have missed more than nine thousand shots, I have lost almost three hundred games, on twenty-six occasions

I have been entrusted to take the winning shot, and I missed. I have failed over and over again in my life, and that is why I succeed.

—Michael Jordan—

You probably know him because of his home run record of 714 during his career, but along with all those home runs came a pretty hefty amount of strikeouts. When asked about this he simply said, "Every strike brings me closer to the next home run."

—Babe Ruth—

*I*t saddens me when children come into my office and are unwilling to persist because they are afraid to fail. A child, afraid of failing? Yes. Many children and teens have a fear of letting down loved ones and themselves.

The first step is to assure them failure is good. Many adults don't realize that either; but it is good to fail before you succeed. Failure is only failure if you don't make an additional attempt. I have a sign in my office that reads, "It doesn't matter how many times you get knocked down; it's how many times you get back up." Once a child accepts the fact that it is okay to fail, they usually excel at what they were trying to accomplish.

I coached a young man in his early twenties who wouldn't work toward his goal because everyone thought it was a crazy goal. His parents continually told him it was too big of a goal and unheard of. That is the problem many have with goal setting. A good goal is one everyone should laugh at. If they don't react then it's too easy to achieve. The impossible is possible.

Once we set goals toward achieving this crazy goal he realized it could be accomplished. The first step was reducing it to bite-sized pieces of reality. The resources available to us from around the world are limitless. I began reaching out to my international resources, which aided in the educational process of how it all worked. You just need to find someone else who has accomplished it, and you can model the process. Of course, you tailor it to your specific ideal, but the basic concept is the same.

The same holds true with a child's dream or vision. Don't ever discourage your child from reaching his/her true potential.

A child came to me because adults told him he wouldn't receive a medal in his current sport. They told him he didn't have what it took to pass that particular level. Well, guess what? They were wrong. Once I was able to encourage him to have faith in his abilities, he started believing he could accomplish it. Yes, faith. It was a work in progress, and we utilized many tools and techniques; but he backed it with persistence. He was then motivated enough to persist in reaching that goal.

The day finally arrived when we learned who passed. He did make it, and everyone was shocked, except for him and me. As you can see by now, it is a process. When each step is backed with persistence and faith, anything can be accomplished.

Being persistent requires that you be definite in your decision, and that requires courage. It is a state of mind; therefore, it can be cultivated. With persistence comes success so you must understand what it takes to be persistent and its causes.

- Definite purpose: know exactly what you desire.
- Burning desire: believe you can accomplish it.
- Specialized knowledge: arrange the accurate knowledge you've accumulated.
- Definite plans: create a strategic plan of action.
- Cooperation: connect harmoniously with like-minded individuals.
- Willpower: enforce willpower with faith.
- Habit: be repetitive with habit; habitual repetitiveness eliminates fear.

Napoleon Hill's book *Think and Grow Rich* speaks of the four steps that lead to the habit of persistence.

- A definite purpose backed by a burning desire for its fulfillment.
- A definite plan expressed in continuous action.
- A mind closed tightly against all negative and discouraging influences, including negative suggestions of relatives, friends, and acquaintances.

- A friendly alliance with one or more persons who will encourage one to follow through with both plan and purpose.

These four steps are essential for success. I feel the most difficult is to eliminate the negativity of friends, relatives, and acquaintances.

Be careful the friends you choose for you will become like them.
—W. Clement Stone—

Many of the children I coach fail to persist because of the types, or lack, of friendships they have. Once a child finds that encouraging circle of friends it will make all the difference in their little world. What are the characteristics of good friendships? Well, I believe a good friendship has to have some degree of caring. Caring allows compassion, concern and empathy. With caring will come support.

This is very important in friendship. It's the balance of the highs and lows. You need to encourage them to look for friends with common interests. This will provide a mutual understanding between the children and will pave the way for loyalty within that friendship. It will result in an honest and trustworthy friend.

All friendships will encounter conflict, so you teach your child how to resolve conflict before it gets out of control. Teach your child that conflict appears as defeat in the friendship. Those who have accepted defeat only as temporary will then add persistence, and this will only result in victory. Successful people fail more often than unsuccessful people. Their failures provide them with the experience and wisdom they need to succeed. Most successful people admit they have learned more from their failures than from their successes.

Many sources have documented that when Thomas Edison was asked if he ever felt disheartened at so many failures he replied that none of his attempts was a failure. They were successful experiments in finding what didn't work, and each one brought him closer to what would work.

When we talk of success, most people think of adults. But if you begin applying the success principles when your children are young and impressionable you teach them how to realize failure is good.

Persistent action comes from persistent vision. When you define your goal and your vision remains exact you will be more consistent and persistent in your actions. That consistent action will produce consistent results.

Napoleon Hill had a famous quote.

Every failure brings with it the seed of an equivalent advantage.

Failure is feedback letting you know what modifications you must make in your plan. Without it you wouldn't have a direction. So expect it and welcome it. Teach your child that he/she may have to make some adjustments, but keep moving and keep persisting.

I've discussed many facts related to the subconscious mind. Please remember that the subconscious mind will translate into reality a thought driven by fear just as readily as it will translate into reality a thought driven by faith. I want you to understand what causes a lack of persistence. The following are the leading causes of failure, which is clearly the lack of persistence:

- Procrastination. This is nothing more than an excuse/an alibi/putting off until tomorrow what we can do today/bargaining for a penny. It's effortless when we can blame others or circumstances instead of taking our own responsibility toward effort or lack of effort in self-discipline.
- Lack of interest in acquiring specialized knowledge. I consider this laziness. It is much easier to surrender to defeat than to obtain the required, educated information for success.
- Indecision. This is being unable to acquire a definite purpose.
- Failure to fight opposition. This is the willingness to give up/surrender.
- Lack of organized planning. This is the absence of organizational skills combined with specialized knowledge for attaining a specific plan of action.

- Failure to move on ideas or opportunities. This is the reluctance to put forward a specific plan of action.

Wishing instead of willing. This is the dreamer who lacks the ambition to turn a dream into a burning desire reinforced with faith.

Attempting to get without giving a fair equivalent. This is selfishness/one who wishes to gain without a price/ the taker.

Fear of criticism. This is someone who is afraid to be judged by others/lacking a sense of self-worth.

Discouragement. This is the most dangerous of all feelings. The separation (only by the width of the word) between success and failure. In my research numerous individuals have mentioned a story associated with discouragement. I placed it in my first book, and I would like to share it with you in this one as well.

There is an old-time fable that the devil once held a sale and offered all the tools of his trade on the table, each one labeled: hatred, malice, envy, despair, sickness and sensuality – all the weapons that everyone knows so well. But, off on one side, apart from the rest, lay a harmless looking, wedge-shaped instrument marked "Discouragement." It was old and worn looking, but was priced far above all the rest. When asked the reason why, the devil replied: "Because I can use this one so much more easily than the others. No one knows that it belongs to me, so with it I can open doors that are tight bolted against the others. Once I get inside I can use any tool that suits me best."

Help your children counter discouragement with encouragement. Success is a wondrous feeling of accomplishment that everyone should be able to experience, but helping attain that in adolescence will make a huge impact on them as adults.

Share historical stories with your children about the successful men of all times. Be sure they understand persistence brought them to victory.

The disparity between failure and success can be bridged by perseverance and faith. Remember to teach your children the difference between the person who fails and the one who succeeds is the perception they have. It is seizing an opportunity and acting upon it, unlike the person who allows fear to dominate his abilities.

And now. . .
teach them how to be grateful.

Chapter 7

The Powerful Outcome Of Gratitude

No one has yet fully realized the wealth of sympathy, kindness and generosity hidden in the soul of a child. The effort of every true education should be to unlock that treasure.

—**Emma Goldman**—

Booted from drama class for being too shy.

—**Lucille Ball**—

More than one thousand rejections and told it was
undeniably the chicken recipe no one wanted.
—**Harland David Sanders** and KFC's Secret Recipe—

I was coaching an older child whose depression and negative emotions developed because children had provoked him with harmful comments about Santa Claus and Christmas. The child came from a wonderful family who unfortunately had encountered a financial setback due to loss of employment. Some classmates bullied the child by planting a seed in his mind that Santa Claus didn't like him because he didn't receive many presents and the ones he did receive weren't worth as much as theirs.

The child carried that around in his mind, and even when he realized Santa Claus was Mom and Dad the mental damage had been established. So, as parents, this can be very controversial. The family experiencing financial difficulties experience heartache due to comparisons with the families who can afford more. And on the other hand, why should the family who can afford elaborate gifts be penalized for those who are unable? Well, you shouldn't be; but turn the situation into a positive. Make it a win-win for everyone.

Christmas can be conveyed to all in a very special manner. Teach your children not to brag to the ones who are less fortunate. Make your elaborate gifts be a family celebration, and if spoken of outside the home have that particular gift be from Mom and Dad and make Santa's gifts the less expensive. Teach your children gratitude and love. Teach them how to give.

From childhood to adulthood I've instilled the gift of giving and gratitude in my own children. When they were young I would encourage them at Christmas to give a gift that would have been for them or save their money and purchase a gift for someone less fortunate.

As they became older we would participate in the Salvation Army's Angel Tree Program and eventually started our own. I would give to someone in need throughout the year and tried to teach them that it's not just about giving gifts. You need to help someone in need.

In my first book I wrote of a certain scenario I would like to share with those of you who haven't read it. While owning one of my businesses I had an exceptional employee. My children were sixteen and nineteen at the time. This employee would go out of his way for the business and for me, and my children definitely recognized it. The individual had two jobs, did not have a vehicle and would ride a bike to work. No matter what the weather was like, my employee was never late.

My daughter was about to pass down her vehicle to my son. He was sixteen years old and excited to receive this vehicle. But he decided to give the vehicle to this employee. It bothered him that someone could work two jobs and have to ride a bike to work. He said he would work additional hours to save enough money to purchase a different vehicle, and he did. He worked enough to purchase a car and a computer for college. That's my gratitude story, and it's my favorite. To think a child at that age could put aside his own desire for the benefit of another. I am grateful.

Taking things for granted and failing to be grateful for the "smaller" delights in life is similar to resistance vs. persistence.

Let me give you the most wonderful example of a video I came across called "The Seven Wonders of the World." If you haven't had the opportunity to see it, I recommend you look it up on YouTube. The story goes like this:

A group of students was asked to list what they thought were the seven wonders of the world. Most voted were:

- Egypt's Great Pyramid
- Taj Mahal
- Grand Canyon
- Niagara Falls
- Empire State Building
- St. Peter's Basilica
- Great Wall of China

While gathering the votes, the teacher noted that one quiet student hadn't turned in her paper yet. She asked her if she was having trouble. The girl replied, "Yes, a little. I couldn't quite make up my mind because there were so many." The teacher said, "Well, tell us what you have and maybe we can help."

The girl hesitated then said she thinks the seven wonders of the world are:

- To touch
- To taste
- To see
- To hear

She hesitated again then added:

- To feel
- To laugh
- To love

The room was so full of silence you could have heard a pin drop. Those things we overlook as simple and ordinary are truly wondrous. A gentle reminder for all of us that the most precious things in life cannot be bought; they must be experienced.

With children the challenge is to make it fun. You must also try to make it fun for your teenagers even though sometimes they will resist. They may get bored easily and be naturally lazier in their minds. Once they begin, they usually have fun and see the benefit. The following are a few ideas to help them with gratitude:

- Write sticky notes and hang them on the mirror. As stated in previous chapters, visualization is a great way to assist with implanting positivity in the subconscious mind. A great start would be to write it out, perhaps on a sticky note, then post it where it will be visible.

- Make space for thanks. Get an erase board and hang it on the outside of the door. Encourage family members to post positive statements on the board. It will bring a smile to your child's face.
- Studies show that smiling has many benefits.
- When you see someone smile it activates the area of your brain that controls your facial movement, which leads to a grin. Most people mimic the expression, even in bad situations.
- It has multiple health benefits and is used to calm people down in stressful situations. It has also been found to lower a person's heart rate.
- My favorite: Smiling releases endorphins that decrease stress and anxiety. Endorphins are the same chemicals you get from working out or running, known as a runner's high.
- You will be more attractive and suggest that you are a personable, easy-going, and empathetic person.
- Smiling strengthens your immune system. The Mayo Clinic is one of many to promote this theory.
- You are considered more social. Those who can easily engage in social settings are usually smiling, which makes them more inviting and shows you are willing to interact easily with others.
- Smiling makes you feel more comfortable in awkward situations.
- Smiling helps you seem more trustworthy.

- Most important, smiling makes you a leader. It shows you're in a position of power, and it could be the key to your success. Studies have shown that smiling is a more effective leadership technique than having great management skills.

Smiling boosts your mood. You will be healthier, feel better and be viewed as more trustworthy and a natural born leader. Why would you not want to smile?

- Do a basket of thank-you notes for whenever your children are thankful for things you've done.
- Gratitude journal. I have all of my clients participate in this one, whether they are executive clients, stay-at-home moms or children. Ask them to write ten things they are grateful for each day.

"I am so happy and grateful for. . . ."

- With gratitude comes giving. Have them give two gifts each month to someone who truly deserves it.
- Have a no-complaining day, which helps keep them positive and removes any chance for negativity to enter their minds.
- Do a grateful jar that would include the following: a special, funny family memory or what they love about a family member.

- Volunteer to help someone. It is good for them to understand that to receive you must give, and volunteering to help someone else can fill them with a sense of gratitude.

Now it's time for you to find out...
the true potential of your child.

Chapter 8

What Is The Real Potential
Of Your Child?

Children are our most valuable resource.
—**Herbert Hoover**, thirty-first US president—

He went broke five times, and Newsweek stated he went out of business because of customer complaints of high prices and low quality.
—**Henry Ford**—

He couldn't wait on customers at a dry goods store because his boss said he lacked the sense to do so.
—F. W. Woolworth—

*L*ost and alone, she felt deep anger, sadness and unworthiness. She put up a wall that would not accept any positive emotions. She had been bullied in school, encountered multiple family issues and was now feeling as though she had nothing to contribute to the outside world. She began by saying, "I'm stupid. The kids in school think I am ugly, stupid and weird. My parents told me I would never work. I have no skills."

Spending so much time alone, she began cutting herself, creating a nightmare of evil thoughts in her head. She felt as if she had no purpose.

There they are again, the horrible scars of bullying and limited beliefs. How do you break through those types of barriers? It isn't easy. Her subconscious mind created a map of reality that was leading her to destruction. I had to reprogram her way of thinking, build her self-esteem, teach her what is wonderful and what to be grateful for and, most important, what skills she possessed. She has wonderful talents and abilities. Her thought process regarding that fact was masked by abuse. It truly is a process. Repetitiveness, desire, faith, visualization, and persistence are the beginning.

Why is discovering your skill sets so important?

We need to prepare our children for this unpredictable world by teaching them how to adapt to any situation. This is in addition to our educational process and is a totally different approach, which requires reinventing everything and leaving our old ideas and habits at the door. A good essential set of skills will best prepare them for any future.

What are the essential steps in discovering your child's skill set?

First of all, you begin by asking questions, a lot of questions. In the developmental years we get frustrated when children ask so many questions. Try to encourage it and utilize the concept of the modeling period in yourself and begin to ask them questions. Understand? Model their own behavior. This is very effective.

Utilizing the modeling period will also teach your child how to solve problems instead of your attempting to solve them. This provides self-confidence. They need to discover strengths and weaknesses, and this will surely deliver your results. Solving problems is also a necessity in goal setting, and, like adults, all children should have goals. Upon discovering problem-solving techniques, they will want to set goals and tackle their own projects.

How would your children know how to begin goal setting?

What are they passionate about? What gives them that excited feeling? Even if you do not feel what they have chosen is the right choice for them, please do not discourage them; but instead encourage them. Just because you don't feel it's right for them doesn't mean it isn't. How many times do you see children grow up to choose the same field as the parent? Why? Is it their love and passion or the parents'? Let them find their own.

This creates independence within the child. They need to learn how to manage their own strengths and weaknesses. Almost everyone who comes to me, whether child or adult, fears failure. I encourage it. Failure is just feedback letting you know how to modify your plan. I truly believe you can't be successful until you have failed. It encourages people to use their so-called failures as stepping stones to success. Remember that failure is only failure when you don't get back up and try again. All of the successful people in history have had many failures before reaching success, and they all say they weren't failures at all. Again I use Edison. Most people would have given up or felt as though they had ten thousand failures while he found ten thousand ways a light bulb wouldn't work. It's all about perception.

In today's society most parents worry too much about their children and coddle them instead of allowing them to figure things out on their own. If children learn from an early age that they can find happiness by playing, reading positive material, being grateful or dreaming, they will have discovered a very valuable skill.

I use the modeling period most in my examples because in working with so many children it is evident this is the most influential period. Remember to model compassion as well with your child. While attending an event for my grandson I observed many sad behaviors of parents allowing their children to be mean to others. They chanted names to root for a popular child or made negative remarks about another child's project. My daughter pulled her son aside and pointed out those things. She asked him to put himself in the place of the child who had been ridiculed. My grandson did not partake in the negative activity, but she still brought the scenario to his attention. I was very impressed to see that.

I also listened to one child, a victim, talking to his parent about how hurt he was. He was even beginning to cry. But the father asked him firmly if he thought he had done a good job on the project, and the child replied, "Yes." The father then told him that was all that mattered. I thought that was wonderful. I wish more parents would be cognizant of their child's behavior.

With compassion you get empathy for other people and belongings. I've personally seen children be mean to animals because they lacked empathy, so modeling compassion with your child is a key factor.

As children grow they need to learn how to deal with change. Changes in circumstances, cultures, and religions help our children to adapt in society. We can't give our children a blueprint in life, but we can teach them coping skills. Your children's skills and abilities will be their most valuable asset throughout their lives.

What are skills and abilities?

Skills are behaviors in which we increase our knowledge, and abilities are natural talents. Understanding what skills and abilities they have and what they need to reach their dreams is an important component in your child's career development.

From childhood your child will develop skills that will be transferred as an adult. Emotional skills such as self esteem, sociability, integrity and empathy, integrated with the educational skills of reading, writing, mathematics, speaking, creativity and decision making will prepare them for adaptability within the corporate world.

What types of skills should they develop?

The following is a breakdown by category:

Personality. Relationship/interaction skills; interpersonal communication. This establishes productive and positive relationships, increases well-being and satisfaction of others and assists toward personal growth. It enables someone to demonstrate behavior and sensitivity, resolve conflict, reinforce compassion and create rapport.

Communication. Exchange of information through verbal, nonverbal and written means. Provides influence and ideas, identifies problems, provides suggestions and develops solutions. The ability to listen, speak, write, edit, sell, consult and negotiate.

- How can I help my child with personality and communication skills? Read to your child; let your child read to you; encourage good listening techniques; play games involving reading, writing, speaking and listening; and encourage writing. Games such as charades will also communicate behavioral and nonverbal skills.

Involve them in family decisions that are age and maturity appropriate. Work on giving them chores to do and place emphasis on working together as a family.

Common. Analytical; logical processing of data to produce information in problem solving, numerical and statistical calculation, and the compilation and organization of data for planning and effectiveness. It is the ability to evaluate, analyze, research, forecast, compute, estimate, and utilize data management.

Creative. Generating ideas and information. The ability to develop perceptions and express a vision into a creative or artistic form.

- How can I help my child with common and creative skills? Cooking together will teach a child how to follow a recipe (fractions and measuring); shopping will illustrate percentages with pennies and dollars (price comparisons); travelling will assist with navigation; playing games will aid in learning rules and reading and enforcing directions.

Physical/Technical. Interaction of the body with physical objects including machinery and technological systems. It is the ability to use one's hands and body with precision. It is being proficient in product assembly and the proper use of tools, hardware, software and equipment. It is body coordination, hand dexterity, building/construction skills, outdoor skills and artistic skills such as art, writing and singing.

- How can I help my child with physical and technical skills? Have them assist with small repairs and play games that involve art, such as drawing, sketching, singing and writing. Allow them to do a project in which they must put something together and encourage them to brainstorm solutions.

Another way to discover and enhance your child's skill set is to have them involved in extracurricular activities. The busier you keep your child the less idle time they have to stumble upon trouble. Getting them involved in sports or activities as a toddler may give them an opportunity to be on an elite team when they are older. Also, many studies have supported the fact that the faster children develop skills, the better they do with testing.

In case you are not familiar with the 4 Cs, I will list them for you. Today's students are moving beyond the basics and embracing the 4 Cs super skills for the twenty-first century. Every child needs twenty-first century knowledge and skills to succeed as effective citizens, workers and leaders. There is a profound gap between the knowledge and skills most students learn in school and the knowledge and skills they need in twenty-first century communities.

The 4 Cs are the skills needed for success in education, career and life:

- Communication—sharing thoughts, questions, ideas and solutions.
- Collaboration—working together to reach a goal; putting talent, expertise and smarts to work.
- Critical thinking—looking at problems in a new way; linking learning across subjects and disciplines.
- Creativity—trying new approaches to get things done equals innovation and invention.

Paul Tough, author of *How Children Succeed,* writes: "Character is created by encountering and overcoming failure." He discusses "the cognitive hypothesis" as the belief that success today depends primarily on cognitive skills—the kind of intelligence that is measured on I.Q. tests. It includes the ability to recognize letters and words, to calculate, to detect patterns; the best way to develop these skills is to practice them as much as possible, beginning as early as possible.

In his new book he sets out to replace this assumption with what might be called "the character hypothesis": the notion that noncognitive skills, like persistence, self-control, curiosity, conscientiousness, grit and self-confidence, are more crucial than sheer brainpower to achieving success.

Prime your children's motivation by connecting learning to their interests and skills, engage them in problem solving, and draw attention to the knowledge and skills students are developing, rather than to their grades.

*Now. . .take their skills and passions
and teach them the entrepreneurial way.
It's time to be a Kidpreneur!*

Chapter 9

How To Turn Your Children Into "Kidpreneurs" And Teach Them The Power Of Masterminding

I continue to believe that if children are given the necessary tools to succeed, they will succeed beyond their wildest dreams.

—**David Vittner**, US senator—

The first year of her contract she was dropped by her producers because they thought she was unattractive and couldn't act.

—**Marilyn Monroe**—

Before the start of his career, his music teacher once said of him, "As a composer, he is hopeless." And during his career he lost his hearing; yet he managed to produce great music. A deaf man composing music—ironic, isn't it?

—**Ludwig Van Beethoven** —

*S*itting in a chair across from my desk is a very enthusiastic child who is about to participate in Children in Business, a local event sponsoring children who have created a business. It was great to see the excitement and to motivate them toward the entrepreneurial world. Discovering skill sets and combining them with passion delivered a business mindset.

Several of my clients participated, and each one was very enthusiastic. They found their talent and combined it in a way that would generate income for them. We had items for sale that included para cord bracelets, duct tape purses and wallets, paintings, and homemade musical instruments.

I teach ways to create multiple sources of income at any age. Educating children and teens about employment or entrepreneurship has astounding affects. It teaches them time management, assists them in learning how to follow directions, and provides team and leadership skills. Studies show discouraged teens often grow up to become discouraged adults. This affects their confidence level in the workforce.

Money lessons are very important. Start teaching as young as age three. I began with my grandson at age four. I gave him a fifty-dollar bill and told him to find a way to double it in a year and then triple it the following year. Once he tripled it I told him to separate it into three jars. The first is a savings jar in which he will save a percentage, the second jar will be the spending jar where he is allowed to spend a percentage, and the last jar is the sharing jar in which he will give the remaining percentage to charity. Think of the lessons each jar will teach him.

You can also use the reward system in which you can match a certain amount. This is much better than just buying them what they want. If they implement the jar exercise and complete their chores then they deserve compensation.

When your children reach age six you should explain that it's important to make wise money choices. They need to understand that if they spend it all there will be none left and they would have to start over in the process. The money jar concept integrates with goal setting and decision making.

Give your children two dollars in a store and see the choices they make. Also, ask good money conscious questions that pertain to decision making. "Is this something you really need?"

Once they reach the age of eleven you can educate them on saving money and how their money can grow from compound interest. Explain concepts that involve saving a certain amount each year and include compound interest by using a certain interest rate. Then do the calculations to show what they would accumulate by age sixty-five. This is where you shift their way of thinking from short-term goals to long-term goals.

You can give them some ideas on jobs that will earn them money. Here are a few examples:

- Babysitting
- Dog walking
- Errand runner
- Making pet treats or dishes
- Designing homemade cards
- Making scrapbooks
- Making friendship bracelets
- Knitting scarves and hats
- Serving food at parties
- Baking cookies
- Collecting and selling
- Cleaning up after parties
- Raking leaves
- These are just a few ideas. Build from them. Be creative!

Once they reach age fourteen you can get them into the financial mindset associated with college. Use a net price calculator on college websites to see how much each costs when including other expenses besides tuition. Instead of letting them think you will pay for their college, allow them to understand the associated costs.

Also explain how there are other ways to assist, such as financial aid, grants and scholarships, and the differences in what needs to be paid back and what is free money. Teaching the fundamental principles at an early age will make them aware of why they need to focus on getting good grades and how their GPA affects the financial status regarding college.

Understanding finance will also help them understand how student loan debt could affect their lifestyle after graduation. This will make them aware of the importance of good spending habits during their college years. Children who help repay their college debt learn to be grateful and conscientious about money. Studies have shown that when children pay a portion of their debt they are generally more focused on their academic performance.

Studies have also shown that children who get a part-time job, working twenty hours per week or less while attending college, received better grades because they were more engaged in student life. But working more than twenty hours per week can affect academic performance. You need a balance.

Teaching children about credit card debt before they go to college is truly beneficial to their lifestyle and yours.

Educate them on the responsibilities of a parent co-signing on a loan or credit card. Any late payment could also affect the parent's credit history. Together look for a low interest rate and no annual fee by using sites like Bankrate.com, Creditcards.com, Credit.com, or Cardratings.com.

Explain how credit cards, when used properly, can help them build good credit. You get to use OPM, which stands for other people's money, for thirty days, and it's interest free if you pay it off when the bill comes in.

Teenagers can find many kinds of work, such as waitressing, retail, lifeguard or golf caddy. But they can also start a small business. Here are a few ideas:

- Social media consultant
- Web design
- Etsy retailer
- Tutor
- House sitting
- Cleaning homes
- Organizing homes
- Painting
- Mowing lawns
- Shoveling snow
- Nanny services
- Entertaining kids at birthday parties
- Assisting kids with school projects
- Setting up new technology
- Blogging for money
- Social media management

- Detailing cars
- Parking cars for parties
- Being a designated driver

They could create a small business with any of these ideas. Again be creative!

Many parents ask what they shouldn't do for their children. Don't suffer the consequences of their mistakes. It is natural for parents to want to protect their children forever, but they need to develop their own sense of responsibility.

Don't cover all their rent and expenses. Suze Orman, personal financial guru, says that while you may not be ready to put your adult child out on the street, it's just as important to take care of your own retirement needs. She suggests that adult kids who move back home be asked to pay rent, however small the amount and however broke the adult child. Even a little something helps them establish a sense of standing on their own two feet.

The advice to take care of yourself first is fairly universal. You have to make sure your own oxygen mask is secure and fastened before assisting your child. Adult children living under your roof need to have rules. Also, be sure they help with house cleaning, grocery shopping and laundry.

The most important message in this chapter and throughout this book is teaching them the importance of failure. Part of the prevention is working with like-minded individuals or masterminding.

What is masterminding?

This is something you, as the parent, should apply and teach to your child or teen.

The concept of the master mind group was formally introduced by Napoleon Hill in the early 1900s. In his timeless classic "*Think and Grow Rich*" Hill describes the master mind principle, : "the coordination of knowledge and effort, in a spirit of harmony, between two or more people, for the attainment of a definite purpose." And "no two minds ever come together without thereby creating a third, invisible intangible force, which may be likened to a third mind."

He explains:

"Energy is Nature's universal set of building blocks, out of which she constructs every material thing in the universe, including man, and every form of animal and vegetable life. Through a process, which only Nature completely understands, she translates energy into matter."

"Nature's building blocks are available to man in the energy involved in thinking. Man's brain may be compared to an electric battery. It absorbs energy from the ether, which permeates every atom of matter and fills the entire universe."

"It is a well-known fact that a group of electric batteries will provide more energy than a single battery. It is also a well-known fact that an individual battery will provide energy in proportion to the number and capacity of the cells it contains."

"The brain functions in a similar fashion. This accounts for the fact that some brains are more efficient than others and leads to this significant statement: A group of brains coordinated, or connected, in a spirit of harmony will provide more thought-energy than a single brain, just as a group of electric batteries will provide more energy than a single battery."

"Through this metaphor it becomes immediately obvious that the master mind principle holds the secret of the power wielded by men who surround themselves with other men of brains."

"There follows now another statement which will lead still nearer to an understanding of the psychic phase of the master mind principle: When a group of individual brains are coordinated and function in harmony, the increased energy created through that alliance becomes available to every individual in the group." Henry Ford began his business career under the handicap of poverty, illiteracy and ignorance. In a short period of ten years he made himself one of the richest men in America. He formed acquaintances with Edison, Firestone, Burroughs, and Burbank, providing additional evidence in the power that is produced through harmonious minds."

"Economic advantages may be created by any person who surrounds himself with the advice, counsel and personal cooperation of a perfect harmony. This form of cooperative alliance has been the basis of nearly every great fortune."

"Andrew Carnegie surrounded himself with a group of fifty men for the definite purpose of manufacturing and marketing steel. He attributed his entire fortune to the power he accumulated through this master mind." – Napoleon Hill's, *"Think and Grow Rich."*

Master-mind groups create a win-win situation for all who participate by developing new friendships and business opportunities. The interaction of the participants creates energy and provides commitment and excitement.

A master-mind group:

- Challenges each other to create and implement goals then holds you accountable.
- Allows you to brainstorm ideas and provide support backed with total honesty, respect and compassion.
- Promotes growth and expansion in your business and personal life.

The agenda belongs to the group, and each person's participation is key because you rely on their feedback, brainstorm new possibilities and set up accountability structures that keep you focused and on track. The possibilities are endless and will move you to greater heights for growth and improvement in your business and personal life. I have been involved with three different master mind groups throughout my life, and the results were amazing. Imagine placing Einstein, Ford, Edison, and the Wright Brothers in a master-mind group? The organized and intelligently directed knowledge could lead to infinite possibilities.

You need to ensure their commitment level is high because if some of the individuals don't participate on a continual basis the outcome is ineffective. When someone fails to participate it decreases the energy flow. If members are unable to attend a meeting you should put a rule in place that they must notify other members prior to the meeting; then whoever is note taker can ensure they receive minutes of the meeting to keep them updated. It takes a few meetings to form a relationship and understand what each member is involved in. It is always helpful to send a picture and short bio of yourself to everyone in the group. It gives you a head start on forming a relationship. You need to choose a time that will be effective for everyone; sometimes that is difficult because of the variances in time zones (especially if they are outside the United States).

Try to keep the size of the group at five to six people. Try to choose people with the following qualities:

- Similar interests: like minded; if you are a self-employed business owner you should seek others who have a similar background.
- Similar success levels: this ensures continuity when seeking sound business or personal advice.
- Strong desire to succeed: they generally inspire you toward motivation and determination.
- Supportive: usually passionate about life and career.

Upon forming the team, coordinate when to meet, usually once a week on the same day and time. You can meet in person or via phone. Once you begin the call, you designate the following:

- Leader: oversees the meeting, keeps things proceeding in an orderly fashion, reads the master-mind principles at the beginning and assigns duties for the next week.
- Note taker: writes down minutes in a summarized manner and types and e-mails them to the group before the next meeting.
- Time keeper: keep the meeting moving so each person has a specified time frame. Allow one minute per person to announce the wins for the week; the remainder of the time is divided by how many people are on the call. Each call should last one hour.

You are probably asking yourself how you could possibly benefit by forming a master-mind group. It is empowering, and the benefits can't be received with a college degree or measured by money. You gain a relationship that provides:

- experience
- skill
- confidence
- progression in your business and personal life
- an instant and valuable support network

- opportunities for creating multiple sources of income
- a sense of shared endeavor
- marketing
- and a wealth of new ideas for solving existing problems and creating new growth and development

How can this benefit children and teens?

Along with the above benefits, it will help them with communication skills, prohibit negativity from negative school experiences, such as bullying, and keep them focused and on track. They are able to brainstorm with other children their age. They can discuss friendship difficulties, bullying issues and parental issues, or it will aid in decision making and goal setting.

You, as the parent, can assist them with setting it up. Schedule meeting times at your house and manage the meeting. Once they gain control of the procedure, leave the room and allow them to brainstorm among themselves.

The groups I've been involved in were made up of individuals from all over the world. Although the principles were originally intended for adults, I have discovered a profound benefit of applying them to children and teens. It allows them to discover their creative abilities, and with social media affecting communication skills this is a process that reinforces personal interaction.

Begin by finding other parents who are interested in developing this creativity in their own child and coordinate who should be on the team. Be sure you let your child be involved in the entire process. Be the first to implement this in your community.

Don't be afraid to fail—be afraid not to try!
Finally. . .let's put it all together.

Chapter 10

Working Together To Create Successful Results

There are no secrets to success. Don't waste time looking for them. Success is the result of perfection, hard work, learning from failure, loyalty to those for whom you work and persistence.

—Colin Powell—

He failed sixth grade and was defeated in every election for public office until he became prime minister at age sixty-two.

—Winston Churchill—

He lost his job and lost eight elections; his fiancé died,
and he had a nervous breakdown.

—**Abraham Lincoln**—

each child who enters my office has encountered some area of difficulty. You're so sweet, so innocent, just trying to understand the saboteurs of life. You ask yourself, Why me? What have I done to deserve this? I'm a great person. Why are others mean to me?

No, it isn't fair, but unfortunately it's what many children endure.

- Are you bullied?
- Are you filled with fear, worry and doubt?
- Are you subjected to abuse and neglect?

You ask:

- Will you help me?
- Will you build my self-esteem?
- Will you eliminate my fears?
- Will you teach me how to be positive and learn to laugh?
- Will you help me with my bad habits?
- Will you believe in me?
- Will someone learn to love me?
- Will you help me get better grades?
- Will you get rid of my anxiety?

- Will you take away my anger and sadness?
- Will you help me make friends?

To the children—yes, yes!

Why? Because I believe in you and I care. Those of you who know me understand that. Those of you who don't, it's never too late to find someone who will help you get back on track in a positive manner. Some care and genuinely want to help. Changing your life begins with knowing and understanding who and what you are. It begins with choices and taking full responsibility for your life.

To the parents of the children—yes, yes! Why? Because you recognize a problem exists or maybe it's the fact that you are trying to prevent it. I can help you help your child.

If you want to change your life you must change your mind.

I can't say it any better than that. Thoughts produce feelings, and feelings produce actions. If you want to change your actions, you must change your thoughts. When you are enthusiastic and positively happy, you send out that same vibration. No matter what you are experiencing, there is a solution. I hope you realize the difference between the conscious and subconscious minds and how powerful they are.

I have encountered a client who experienced all of the above: neglect, abandonment, abuse, bullying. This left her with a sense of distrust, fear, worry, doubt, anger, sadness, negativity and lack of self-esteem. It was one of the worst cases I have ever seen. Applying the entire coaching process and understanding behavioral patterns I was able to make a huge difference and help her finally reach success.

- Let's recap the chapters and discover how each one helped the child.

Who And What Are Manipulating Your Child's Mind?

Understanding the complexities of the subconscious mind is the first step in helping a child. Your conscious mind makes the choices (the reasoning mind), and the subconscious mind accepts what is impressed upon it or what you consciously believe. The other important component is that the subconscious mind cannot differentiate between positive and negative and both can't occupy the mind at the same time; one must dominate.

What is a hidden saboteur in your child, and how do you recognize it? Is it divorce, stepfamilies, bullying, social media, friends or technology? Once you recognize it, determine the effect it is having on the child physically and emotionally. Understand the different levels throughout your child's life so you can identify how he or she processes information.

We've discussed the various ways to access your child's subconscious mind and how you defeat resistance. Understanding how to recognize negative impressions and replace them with repetitive positive phrases will begin the process toward a successful outcome. Equally important is the power of autosuggestion and positive affirmations. Eliminate negativity at all costs.

- Relating this chapter to the above-mentioned story we see that the process began by studying her behavioral patterns and discovering her way of thinking. Understanding which period most of the problems began in helped me realize how difficult a process it would be for change to take place.

- Since she had encountered multiple problems it was evident that each one took place in a different period. Of course, it started in the imprint level because of parental neglect and abuse. But the torment from bullying began in the modeling period, the level after the imprint period.

- Step one would be autosuggestion and positive affirmations; therefore, a hypnotherapy tape might be helpful in accelerating that particular process.

I have a dream that my four little children will one day live in a nation where they will not be judged by the color of their skin, but by the content of their character.
—**Martin Luther King Jr.**—

How To Teach Your Child
The Importance Of Visualization

You've learned that visualization is one of the keys to success. Allow your children to daydream and help them with a vision board. Seeing words on the screen of your mind will surely bring it to life. Teaching relaxation methods will also teach them how to visualize their goals.

Creative imagination is vital to their lives. It is the receiving set of the brain. So use your senses and make it a reality. Making a vision board is a fun exercise for you to do with your children; it will be interesting to see what pictures they use. Have them look at it daily and keep it in their rooms so they can see it when they awake and before going to bed. You can also place pictures on their iPad or iPod where they view it often.

- This chapter relates to the child's story since we recognize the time period in which neglect and abuse began. By applying the process of autosuggestion we could get her involved in the visioneering process. Figuring out strengths and weaknesses and helping her have calmness of mind would open the channels for visualizing.

- The first thing she began to focus her vision on was being what she thought was normal and having friends. At this point, she had never experienced friendship and was labeled at a very young age. But building her self-esteem and showing her she could start over gave her a wondrous feeling—like being born anew. No one in the new school district would know of her background or labeling. She started to get excited about what could be.

- We began a vision board. The first pictures related to beauty products, name brand clothing, hairstyles, fitness and children in socialization groups.

Cherish your visions and your dreams as they are the children of your soul, the blueprints of your ultimate achievements.

—Napoleon Hill—

What Do Your Children Desire, And How Can You Help Them Get There?

Once your children can visualize their goal you must help them achieve it. A big part of almost everyone's problem is fear. Many children are afraid to fail; therefore, it is our job as parents to encourage failure. Remember discussing how failure can be a good thing? You mustn't fear it; instead welcome it. That is how we learn and grow. Failure is feedback letting you know how to modify your plan. Failure is only bad when you don't get back up.

Remember to discuss the most successful people in history. All of them had to make multiple attempts before attaining success. Also refer to the "burn the boats" story. It can help them realize the no-retreat theory. Once you begin you must continue with no looking back. You must win or perish. It will have a psychological impact, build strength and help them realize nothing is impossible.

In the same way burning the child's negative list has a psychological impact. It is symbolic; but the action releases it faster, and the focus on the positive will eventually override all negativity. It takes at least thirty days for changes to occur in the subconscious mind.

Even if your children have smaller desires, have them concentrate on one definite object and one idea at a time. Once they experience that deep burning desire to succeed they become filled with enthusiasm and courage. This is what will accelerate a successful outcome.

- This chapter relates to the child's story by helping her with the concept of fear and how to eliminate it. Teaching her failure has allowed her to focus on success. Teaching her the history of successful people and discussing the "burn the boats" story ignited enthusiasm. We began to set small goals she could easily attain. This would also get her excited that she could accomplish anything she set her mind to.

- She realized the importance of goal setting and started to think of something much larger.

If you raise your children to feel that they can accomplish any goal or task they decide upon, you will have succeeded as a parent and you will have given your children the greatest of all blessings.

—**Brian Tracy**—

What Happens To Your Child When Intuition And Faith Are Applied?

In my coaching experience it has proven successful that once children believe in a higher power they change their way of thinking. When children do not believe in a higher power they think the parents are the highest form; if they disrespect and betray them, then there are no other consequences. The children who have no belief system have nothing to fear. But once they believe there is something bigger they are more aware of defying consequences.

If they do not believe in something it is more difficult to teach gratitude. Think about all the good that comes from gratitude. When you are grateful for something you tend to respect the religious aspect. And the power of positivity is harder to instill in those who have no belief system.

Also, thoughts that are mixed with emotion and faith translate themselves into their physical counterpart. We discussed the seven laws that govern the universe, and, once understood, we become harmonious with our thoughts and actions.

We also help them understand and develop the mental process of intuition, or the sixth sense. It is a mixture of mental and spiritual. Once developed, children will begin to trust their instincts, keeping them out of harm's way. They communicate with their internal mind by involving feelings and learning how to distinguish those genuine feelings of the heart from emotional reactions of the subconscious mind.

- This chapter relates to the child's story by demonstrating that gratitude is empowerment. The child had absolutely no belief system and was not receptive to such teachings. Once progression began and she experienced friendship, questions surfaced about something bigger being out there. We began to focus on the belief of energy. At least it was a beginning and something to believe in.

- With each step of progress she became curious and began to explore options. She researched, listened and started to believe that all the good things had to be helped along by something or someone else. It was a slow process, but eventually she opened her mind to the belief in a higher power—a power for good.

-

There are people in the world so hungry that God cannot appear to them except in the form of bread.
                                        —Gandhi—

Divorce, Separation, Stepchildren, Bullying. . .Help!

Many factors cause a child to internalize their emotions. Not in all cases, but in some, step situations can cause multiple problems. They include favoritism issues within step brothers/sisters, anger between stepparents and child, or divorce. Sometimes in divorce situations the child is allowed to play the parents against one another. This is very common and a terrible mistake. Even though the parents can't live together or remain in a marriage, the key is to stay firm in your parenting. When one parent gives consequences the other parent should honor it. If you don't agree with the punishment it should be discussed when the child is not around.

Unfortunately, in many scenarios, child support plays a factor. Sometimes, but not always, the parent who is paying child support attempts to win the child over so they will want to live with them, therefore, eliminating that financial responsibility. This is detrimental to the child. It would be nice if both parents were required to pay equally for the child. It would make for a more agreeable arrangement.

In my coaching experience with young clients, they have expressed no remembrances of the marriage if the divorce occurred when the child was young. In those instances, the child does not seem to be affected by the divorce. But when it happens in the teenage years there seem to be additional problems. These instances do not exist in all cases. I am just trying to get parents who are divorced to look for behavioral changes and discover why negative changes occur.

There are times, even with teens, that the child is happy for the divorce because of the loud arguments. Most problems surface when the marriage ends and the child was caught off guard. In some circumstances the parents do not display any negativity in front of the child, which is good; but sometimes they fail to talk and explain that problems do exist. Then, when one of the parents moves out, the child is confused. Therefore, as in all relationships, communication is key.

Bullying is far too common and serious. It leaves a very harmful effect on children. Pay close attention to this chapter in my book so you can watch for signs. It has a major impact on your child, and it carries to adulthood. I've mentioned multiple times about being aware if your child is being bullied or if your child is the bully. Please ask the proper questions to make that determination because if it is caught early enough the impact it has on their self-esteem can be repaired quicker.

Social media also plays a significant role in today's society. It is so easy for even the best kids to stumble on pornography. And the online predators stay on top of things so that it is easy to seek children out. I provided a few of the online sites you need to be aware of as well as software to monitor for prevention.

With children of today being so technologically advanced, you must continually educate yourself. Many children know more about technology than parents, so if you don't know how to do it check out the many resources available to help.

- This chapter relates to the child's story in that there were multiple culprits. She felt the negative emotional impact from the divorce and had negative experiences in the stepfamily. Bullying greatly affected her personality, and then she went through exposure on the Internet.

- I needed to help her understand the marital problems were not her fault. She had never experienced the love of a family, just constant animosity.

- Bullying was a bit more complicated. You must rebuild the child's self-esteem. I used many tools and techniques of neurolinguistics programming. This is effective with children, and it modifies behavioral problems. As a professional in that area I was equipped with the educational material required for that modification. You will need the assistance of a professional if that type of therapy is needed. It is better to prevent bullying, because once it has happened the impact is implosive.

- She also kept a journal and did a mirror exercise. The bullying was one of the worst cases I had ever seen. It wasn't just a few kids who bullied her; the majority of the kids in her grade did so. This had a detrimental impact on her self-esteem. It caused fear, worry and doubt about attending school. It also caused her to become enraged inside, and her inability to release emotions became disastrous. Internalizing all that negativity caused her to dislike her personality and appearance, which led to cutting. By her being unable to release anger she began hurting animals.

- I now had to get her to release all of that. We wrote the positive and negative list and then burned the negatives. Again, it was totally symbolic.

But eventually the positive overrides because the negative no longer exists. It's a little like out of sight, out of mind. Focusing on all the good things she now had in her life eventually brought smiles and gratitude. She became a popular girl in school, and that reinforcement also helped build her self-esteem.

- Educating her on Internet safety was next. I've worked with the state police on this issue, so I knew the proper steps to take.
- Understanding where the problems lie, motivating her by concentrating on her desire, incorporating a belief system, and applying techniques is where we are so far. The next step was to get her to be persistent, be grateful, discover what skills she had, focus on the benefits of building a business, and reach for the end result of success.

The world is a dangerous place, not because of those who do evil, but because of those who look on and do nothing.
—Einstein—

Show Your Child How To Persist

Once you know exactly what you want and you are definite in your decision, you need to persist. With persistence comes success. We discussed that the causes of persistence are being definite in your purpose, having a burning desire to succeed, possessing specialized knowledge, developing definite plans, cooperating with like-minded people, having willpower and forming a habit. You must close your mind tightly to all negative influences.

In persistence, it helps to have good friendships. A good circle of friends will prove to be beneficial for your child.

When we talk of success, most people think of adults. But, as we discussed in this chapter, applying the success principles at an early age will certainly be a benefit. Failure was mentioned several times throughout the book; it plays a significant role with persistence. When persistence is applied it helps with fear of failure. That particular fear begins in childhood; if we teach the benefits of it at an early age it will help your child while developing. Remember that "every failure brings with it the seed of equivalent advantage." – Napoleon Hill's, *"Think and Grow Rich."*

Be aware of the leading causes of failure, especially the lack of persistence. Other causes include procrastination, lack of interest in acquiring specialized knowledge, indecision, failure to fight opposition, lack of organized planning, failure to move on ideas or opportunities, wishing instead of willing, attempting to get without giving fair equivalent, fear of criticism and discouragement.

Don't forget to discuss the failures of the most successful people in history. That plays a significant role because they have someone or something to relate failure to.

- This chapter relates to the child's story by teaching her the positive outcome of persisting. Persistence played a key role in her progress. She began to see that positivity could take her in a direction with endless possibilities. She liked the "new me" and realized she was getting a new opportunity with new possibilities.

- The new circle of friends placed her in a very different mindset. This child had had absolutely no friends, and now she enjoys smiles, acts of kindness, whispers and giggling. She wondered, "Wow! What have I missed out on for so long?" She finally started to understand my teachings on failure. When she first came to me, she thought her entire life was a failure, but she had many things to learn.

- From the previous chapters we discussed how many of the processes helped her overcome such a detriment. Once she began to apply each area she realized the importance of persistence. If she learned them but failed to push forward in the application process then she would experience the negatives again. She was empowered to see positive results so she found it easier to keep pushing forward.

Failures are divided into two classes: those who thought and never did, and those who did and never thought.
—**John Charles Salak**, author—

The Powerful Outcome Of Gratitude

An attitude of gratitude!

In today's society we encounter many negative influences and therefore need a positive intervention. Gratitude is so beneficial. You can't reach a higher level until you are grateful for all you have. Being grateful places your child in a positive energy flow and enhances many emotions, such as empathy, happiness, and excitement, and builds great character.

I listed multiple ways to get them involved in the gratitude process. Getting them to become grateful allows them to think about their lives instead of taking so many things for granted, such as physical items and emotional ties. It teaches them the importance of smiling. It is so warm and inviting to see people smile rather than watching them scowl. Being grateful also helps them demonstrate wonderful acts of kindness to others.

- This chapter relates to the child's story by showing the importance of gratitude on many levels. Once the child began to focus on the wonderful things in her life and be grateful for them, she became motivated and empowered to seek out new and wonderful ways of life. Even though burning the negative list was only symbolic, it helped the positives become dominant.

- Looking at the positive list every day and not visually seeing the negative helped her forget the bad. After a month had passed she told me she actually had to think hard to remember anything on the negative list. She had her focus on new friendships and matters of the heart. She was truly grateful she was able to see positive results in her life by applying all the steps of coaching.

• Experiencing spirituality also allowed her to be additionally grateful for a higher power. She began to realize this higher power is a power for good. I am grateful that she is grateful.

As we express our gratitude, we must never forget that the highest appreciation is not to utter words, but to live by them.

—**John F. Kennedy**—

What Is The Real Potential Of Your Children?

Discovering your children's skill sets is vital. It provides them with a sense of value once they realize their capabilities, and it helps them become creative. They need to be able to adapt to any situation, and it is a completely different approach from that of our educational system. It helps eliminate old habits and paves the way for new ones. It enhances problem-solving abilities and plays a key role in goal setting.

It helps you discover not only their talents and abilities, but also their true passion. Once they discover what they are truly passionate about, they become excited, placing them in a positive energy flow. It builds self-confidence and creates independence. It also teaches lessons on failure and allows them to accept failure as stepping-stones.

It helps them deal with cultural changes as well as changes in circumstances. Your children's passions and skills are their most valuable assets in life. Skills are behaviors in which we increase our knowledge, and abilities are natural talents. It is crucial in their career development.

Not only will you discover their skills sets, but you will understand their personality and can teach them better communication skills. You discover their creativity, and it encourages them to become involved in extra-curricular activities. Remember: the less idle time they have, the better.

- This chapter relates to the child's story by demonstrating the importance of finding your hidden talents and abilities. At times we tend to focus on the surface, which is the obvious, but when we reflect deeper we discover areas we weren't even aware of. By performing an exercise to discover skill sets we were able to focus on goals and what the child was truly passionate about. Going through all the horrible experiences in her life left her unable even to think happy thoughts. Her paradigm left her feeling that she had no talents, and her negative energy prohibited her from having the desire to reflect. Once she began to see the positives she was able to reach deep within herself to reveal passion. She knew of several things she loved, but once we truly asked questions and did some soul searching, she recognized alternate areas she was good at—areas that hadn't come to mind until we discovered them. She could then begin to incorporate her skills into goal setting and the visionary process.

The greatest gifts you can give your children are the roots of responsibility and the wings of independence.
—Denis Waitley—

How To Turn Your Children Into "Kidpreneurs" And Teach Them The Power Of Masterminding

Once you've discovered talents, abilities and passions, you are ready to turn them loose to the business side of things. Instilling entrepreneurial ideas in your child will help them become successful as adults. It will also get them thinking creatively in acquiring multiple sources of income. Money lessons are very important.

The reward system is important in multiple areas; in the business arena it teaches children the impact of saving and giving, rather than just spending. I listed many areas in which they could begin earning money as a small business. Also, get them involved in community events that are related to business as in the example in our town of "Kids in Business."

An understanding of money will benefit them when they go to college or build their credit. Paying a portion of their own debt will keep them focused, and they will be more likely to succeed in the corporate world. Also, keeping them focused on employment eliminates that idle time, which can be trouble.

Teach them responsibility in the domestic area, such as laundry, shopping and cleaning. Many parents make the mistake of not allowing their children to assist with domestic chores or finances. This leaves them with a sense of false hope once they get out on their own. It's not being mean; it's preparing them for the world. The more tools you provide them with, the more advanced they will become.

Implement a mastermind team for yourself, as the parent, and one for your child or teen. You will see the miraculous benefits from surrounding yourself with like-minded individuals. It will also reinforce communication and interpersonal relations. It helps with problem solving and accountability, both personally and professionally. When teens begin employment it helps them find solutions in the transition from childhood to adulthood.

- This chapter relates to the child's story by showing how understanding the entrepreneurial world as a child or teen can assist with success as an adult. The child could now focus on her abilities. She realized she could actually build a business as a teenager. It was very encouraging to watch her excitement, and it was very rewarding when she developed a new mindset. She could actually visualize what she could become and then believed very strongly she could make that dream a reality.

- She utilized all the principles of my teaching and worked diligently to apply the processes. It was a lot of effort on her part, but seeing positive results made her even more driven. She realized that the possibilities of this big world are limitless once she believed and then persisted.

- She realized she would encounter many obstacles, but she felt that she could overcome anything because of already dealing with a severe detriment. The risk was now easier because she no longer feared failure. It was just a stepping-stone to success. Failure is only failure when you stop trying.

- She incorporated the masterminding principle, and the group helped her when she encountered difficulties. She loved forming her group, and it has had a profound impact on her. She continually applies all the principles and is succeeding in multiple areas. She is a true success.

Those who educate children well are more honored than they who produce them; for these only gave them life, those the art of living well.
    —**Aristotle**—

Now smile. . .for kindness, honesty, and success are knocking at your door!

Apply each of these principles and begin to understand your child's mind and behavior. Enhance the good and rid the bad. Teach them success.

The price of greatness is responsibility.
                              —**Sir Winston Churchill**—

About the Author

Peggy Caruso is passionate about helping people. She wrote this book to assist parents with being able to identify behavioral and psychological issues in children. She provides details at each level of their adolescence and will guide parents on preventative measures to safeguard their children. Peggy has 100% success rate; which is attributed to her education and personal experiences.

She has 22 years experience, is an 8-time Entrepreneur, the Author of 4 books and has been featured on Women's Radio, Word-of-Mom radio, WHPC, 90.3 in New York, Ask The Expert on WCED and New Living Magazine.

In addition to being an Executive and Personal Development Coach, Peggy is an advanced NLP Master Practitioner and Trainer, Hypnotherapist, and certifies individuals to become a Life Coach. Her education allows her to expand her typical life coaching client base to assist those with ADD/ADHD and depression. She assists in getting children and adults off of their depression medication; which benefits them by recognizing their issues and being able to move forward in a positive direction.

Whether you are an entrepreneur, executive, stay-at-home mom, college student or child, Peggy has the ability to assist you at any level. Thoughts produce feelings, feelings produce actions so if you want to change your actions you must first change your thoughts.

www.lifecoachingandbeyond.com
peg.caruso@lifecoachingandbeyond.com

SCAN THIS CODE
using your mobile device

to view your
FREE GIFTS page

References

Bob Proctor, business consultant, motivational speaker, personal development coach, author, star of the movie *The Secret*. www.bobproctorcoaching.com - law of attraction, universal laws

Dr. Robert Anthony, www.thesecretofdeliberatecreation. com - subconscious mind, developmental periods, critical factor

Dr. Steve G. Jones, hypnotherapist, NLP trainer, author. www.stevegjones.com

Jack Canfield, author, motivational speaker. www. jackcanfield.com

Napoleon Hill, Napoleon Hill Foundation, *Think and Grow Rich*, 1937. www.naphill.org

Oprah Winfrey, television host, *O Magazine,* OWN. www. oprah.com

Paul Tough, writer, broadcaster. www.paultough.com

Suze Orman, American author, financial advisor, motivational speaker and television host. www. suzeorman.com

www.alumni.stanford.edu

www.davidsongifted.org

www.mayoclinic.org

www.naeyc.org

www.ngm.nationalgeographic.com

www.one.min.energy.com

www.psychologytoday.com

www.scientificamerican.com

Printed in the USA
CPSIA information can be obtained
at www.ICGtesting.com
JSHW082343140824
68134JS00020B/1840

9 781630 472528